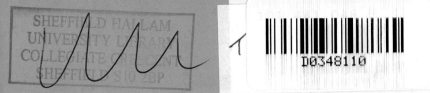

The New Ideology
of Imperialism

Renewing the Moral Imperative

Frank Füredi

Pluto  **Press**

LONDON • BOULDER, COLORADO

Pluto Studies in Racism and Imperialism
by Frank Füredi

The Ambivalent Legacy: British Imperialism in the Twentieth Century

The Hidden Face of Imperialism

First published 1994 by Pluto Press
345 Archway Road, London N6 5AA
and 5500 Central Avenue
Boulder, Colorado 80301, USA

British Library Cataloguing in Publication Data
A catalogue record for this book is available from the British Library

Library of Congress Cataloging in Publication Data
Füredi, Frank. 1947
  The new ideology of imperialism: renewing the moral imperative
Frank Füredi.
  140 p. 22cm. – (Pluto studies in racism and imperialism)
  Includes bibliographical references and index.
  ISBN 0-7453-0845-7
  1. Developing countries–Politics and government. 2. Nationalism–
Developing countries. I. Title. II. Series.
JF80.F87 1994
320.5'4'091724–dc20   93-50843
                                                               CIP

ISBN 0 7453 0845 7 hbk

Designed and Produced for Pluto Press by
Chase Production Services, Chipping Norton
Typeset from author's disks by
Stanford DTP Services, Milton Keynes
Printed in the EC by TJ Press, Padstow

Contents

1 Introduction

The noisy celebrations that accompanied the collapse of the Soviet Empire did not last very long. The rhetoric about a stable and peaceful New World Order was soon accompanied by warnings of a new, unpredictable menace threatening the West. Before long, commentators on both sides of the Atlantic insisted that the Cold War had in fact been a relatively stable interlude. The title of John Mearsheimer's 1990 article 'Why We Will Soon Miss The Cold War' captured the mood of mainstream commentators at the time.[1] Such sober if not pessimistic accounts were combined with predictions of dire dangers ahead for the West. These alarmist reactions were at first unspecific and unclear. But gradually these concerns have become focused around what is termed 'Third World nationalism'.

In the contemporary discussion, the theme of Third World nationalism covers a variety of sins. The term is invoked to describe many of the Western media's hate figures, from Shiite gunmen to Somali warlords through to Castroite guerrillas. The label 'Third World nationalism' is used along with a variety of others – 'fundamentalist', 'terrorist' – without the slightest regard for precision, to describe movements with which the West does not feel comfortable. The intense hostility shown towards these so-called anti-Western movements in the recent period is truly remarkable. If anything, the passion excited by these demons from the Third World surpasses even the frenzied rhetorical exchanges of the Cold War.

There is now a veritable literature devoted to the denigration of the Third World. Political movements from Africa, the Middle East or Latin America are represented in the most unflattering terms. This campaign of abuse is seldom accompanied by any attempt at rational argument. Often the discussion is based entirely on innuendo. For example, in an article ominously headed 'dark spectre chills a bright spring', *Sunday Times* columnist Norman Macrare observed that as 'Bolshevism dies 50 years later, it would be horrid if any nationalism (including African ones) sprang from its graves'.[2] How, even metaphorically, nationalism springs from the Bolshevik grave and why attention is drawn to the African

1

variety is left to the imagination of the reader. Nor does the author explain why such a development frightens him so. It is as if there is no need to elaborate. That Third World nationalism is horrid is assumed to have the status of common sense.

The reaction to Third World nationalism sometimes assumes pathological proportions. 'Blood Hatred' was the title of a 1993 survey by *Newsweek* which reported on 'Africa's tribal animosities'. The London *Times* has suggested that there is an 'inversion of ordinary psychology' when it comes to Islam – in other words, rational criteria can not be applied to this phenomenon. Political Islam, in its view, is a 'pathological over-reaction to the challenges to traditional Islamic cultures'. 'We must confront the fact that black Africa has all but gone back into the dark', exclaimed Tom Stacey in the *Daily Telegraph*. Dark, irrational monsters prowl the world of Islam and Africa. The inescapable conclusion to be drawn from this diagnosis is that the Third World is a stranger to the conventions of civilisation. Such assessments are often combined with calls for the destruction of this transcendent evil. 'An ugly, evil spirit is abroad in the third world and it cannot be condoned: only crushed, as Carthage was crushed by the Romans', wrote the editor of the *Sunday Telegraph*.[3]

The demonisation of the Third World is conducted not only in the press. Academics have often played a full part. In his survey of the twentieth century, the American historian John Lukacs pointedly intimates that the 'one common element' of movements in 'the oddest places of the so-called Third World was a tribal hatred of foreign, in most cases white, power'. The RAND Corporation's Francis Fukuyama shares this disdain for Third World movements. In his *The End of History and the Last Man*, Fukuyama proposes the establishment of a league of civilised nations 'capable of forceful action' to police the Third World.[4] 'Fanatic', 'extremist', 'terrorist' and 'criminal' are the favoured terms used to describe the movements under discussion.

The intensity of the hatred directed towards the Third World is matched by the conviction that it represents the main threat to global stability. It is as if the ideological West–East rivalry of the Cold War has spontaneously given way to an even more ferocious, but this time cultural/racial, West–East conflict. The accepted wisdom in the West today is that the Third World now constitutes the main threat to the world order. In the specialist literature on current affairs, this opinion goes virtually uncontested. The poorest regions in the world, with limited access to technology and other resources and the least power, are mysteriously recast as the greatest danger to humanity. How the powerless could come to be the principal global problem is seldom considered. Banal commentary regarding the sheer weight of population and the unpredictable character of Eastern fanaticism exhausts the argument. The idea that population and fanaticism cannot pose a formidable challenge to the hi-tech weaponry and industry which remains under the monopoly of the West is simply not considered.

The terms used to describe the problem regimes of Africa and Asia are highly ideological. They are 'terrorist states' or 'weapons states'. What seems to concern Western experts, however, is not so much the weapons but the sentiments these states are alleged to harbour. 'The current Weapon States have deep grievances against the West' according to a paper in *Foreign Affairs*. Such grudges are by definition inexplicable and threatening. Ominously, the author hints, 'they are therefore subversive of the international status quo, which they see as a residue of colonialism'. The inescapable conclusion is that the strength of these 'subversive' grievances requires the vigilance of the West. Another contribution on this subject argues that 'nationalism, non-alignment and religious fundamentalism have proved to be of more transcendent importance in the Third World than communism'.[5]

The linking of such diverse concepts as nationalism, non-alignment and religious fundamentalism provides an insight into the thinking behind the demonisation of the Third World. Any expression of autonomy and independence is automatically interpreted as antithetical to the interests of the West. This antithesis is most adequately represented through the cultural framework of a traditional clash of civilisations. The idea of a 'societal cold war', a hi-tech crusade to defend the Western way of life is an important underlying theme in the discussion.[6] 'The Clash of Civilizations?', by the prominent American political scientist and State Department adviser Samuel Huntington provides a useful synthesis of this approach. Huntington recycles Spengler's old thesis and argues that the 'clash of civilizations will dominate global politics'. With one eye on a 'West–Islam conflict', he also fears the coming together of all non-Western interests and the consequent changing balance of power. His argument concludes with the now predictable call for Western military vigilance to defend itself against Eastern civilisations.[7]

Huntington's retreat into the irrational philosophy of the interwar Spengler suggests that many aspects of the discussion are far from new. Throughout this century, anti-colonial and anti-imperial movements have been portrayed in the most unflattering terms. Their motives, idealism and rationality have always been subject to interrogation.

Western commentators have rarely brought themselves to characterise these movements as political – at best they have been the dupes of the Soviet Union or some other foreign manipulator. A study of American foreign policy towards the Third World published in the 1970s described Washington's orientation as 'antinationalist' and one which systematically questioned the legitimacy of movements from that part of the world.[8] As we shall see, this anti-nationalism was fully shared by policy makers in London.

It would be wrong to see the Western hatred of Third World nationalism merely as a timeless recurring theme. Today, more than in the past, it stands out as a singular obsession of Western diplomacy. To grasp fully the dimensions of the contemporary crusade against Third World nationalism it will be necessary for us to examine the history of this obsession. Before that, however, it is important to explore further the content of Western hostility.

Contesting Legitimacy

The core of the problem for the West is the historic coincidence of the crisis of the Western imperial ideal and the assertion of anti-colonial aspirations. By the end of the First World War, Western imperialism had lost its vigour and self-confidence. At the level of ideas the case for Empire had become problematic. As Hans Kohn's path-breaking study of Eastern nationalism argued, the rhetoric of imperialism regarding the civilising mission of Empire was coming into conflict with the demand for autonomy in the colonies:

> the tendency of the colonial peoples to assert their national independence and equal rights is depriving imperialism first of its justification, and afterwards of the possibility of survival. The cultural mission of the West as a basis of its dominance is no longer recognized in the East, and even in the West it is called in question by an increasing number of people.[9]

The rise of anti-colonial aspiration at once called into the question the imperial ideal. Without 'grateful subjects' the idea of Empire could no longer be presented as a benevolent mission.

The inconsistency between Western rhetoric and action was particularly evident during the 1919 Paris Peace Conference. Here US President Woodrow Wilson's affirmation of the principle of national self-determination implied the acceptance of the principle of equality as a factor governing international affairs. In practice the exercise of this principle was heavily qualified. It certainly was not intended for export to Asia or Africa. The beneficiaries of Wilson's largesse were restricted to Europe.

The limits to equality were demonstrated by the West's rejection of Japan's attempt to include a clause on racial equality in the League of Nations Covenant. Western diplomats at Paris and their governments at home perceived the Japanese amendment as a threat. According to one account, the Japanese amendment was 'palpably a challenge to the theory of the superiority of the white race on which rested so many of Great Britain's imperial pretensions'.[10] The West's rejection of the principle of racial equality sat uneasily alongside its affirmation of national self-determination. The tension underlined the internal incoherence of imperialist thought.

Even the formal acceptance of the principle of national self-determination helped to deepen the moral and intellectual crisis of imperialism. On the basis of the European and American experience the association of nationalism with modernity was deeply embedded in Western thought. Along with the industrial revolution, the national revolutions of the eighteenth and nineteenth centuries had marked the West's entry into the modern capitalist age. On the basis of this experience, nationalism as such could not be rejected by Western thinkers, since it was identified as the most significant political manifestation of modernity. As Kohn argued, 'the distinguishing mark of modern times is the notion of nationality and of all that it involves'.[11] Imperialism could not, without renouncing its own culture of modernity, mount an intellectual attack against the claims of nationalism.

The paradox was that, precisely because of the association of nationalism with modernity, it encouraged African and Asian politicians to cast their claims in a national form. No doubt many of them anticipated that the language of nationalism would endow their claim with the authority of an internationally accepted principle. This was exactly what imperialists had feared.

The predicament that faced the West in the interwar period was how to react to anti-colonial claims presented in a nationalist form. Since nationalism constituted an acceptable political standpoint, moreover one that was characteristically *modern*, it was not possible intellectually or ideologically to question its basic premise. Western reactions against Eastern nationalism could be expressed at the level of public rhetoric, but could not be justified through an elaborated system of ideas. For the West to deny to others a principle that it had accepted for itself would smack of hypocrisy and bad faith. And yet to acquiesce in these claims would mean abandoning vital imperial interests and global power.

Acceptance of the principle of self-determination at Versailles in 1919 also undermined the pretensions of the colonial mission. The establishment by the League of Nations of a mandate system implied that the dependent status of a particular people would be temporary. As Mayall argued, by accepting the provisional character of mandates, 'the liberal imperialists had, in effect made the first public admission that empire in and of itself was no longer a legitimate political form'.[12] This further weakened the imperialists' intellectual case against anti-colonial nationalism. Rights which were accepted in principle could not without violating its logic be denied to those who demanded them. The League of Nations attempted to restrict the principle under its Article 22, which justified international trusteeship on the grounds that some states were 'inhabited by peoples not yet able to stand by themselves under the strenuous conditions of the modern world'. However in practice, such qualifications gave way to the growing anti-colonial mood.[13]

The dilemma posed by the assertion of anti-colonial aspirations was resolved in the West not by explicitly questioning the principle of the right of nations to self-determination, but by casting doubts on the claim to what was called *genuine nationalism*. Since nationalism as such could not be directly combatted, its anti-colonial variant had to be confronted in a round-about way. By questioning whether anti-colonial movements were genuinely nationalist, it was possible to discredit the opposition without apparently violating the principle of national self-determination. So the target of imperial propaganda was not the principle of nationalism as such but the illegitimate pretensions of anti-colonial politicians.

One obvious line of argument used in the West was to suggest that modern nationalism could not thrive in the condition of economic backwardness which prevailed in the East. These economic arguments invariably concluded with calls for patience until the time arrived when a traditional society would be ready to exercise the rights associated with a modern nation. Theories of colonial development were elaborated in the 1930s to give substance to the arguments. Although this theme endures to this day, it lacked sufficient force to make a great deal of difference. The attempt to qualify the principle of national self-determination on economic grounds suffers from a flaw in logic. The right to nationhood is not constituted on economic grounds. It is a right which is based on the principles of formal democracy. The introduction of economic qualifications was self-evidently a negation of democracy, since it directly limited the autonomy of the subject to enjoy this right.

A far more effective way of combatting anti-colonial nationalism was by discrediting its claims. According to imperial propaganda, these were not proper nationalists. They were invariably indicted as unrepresentative agitators, criminal subversives, religious fanatics or malevolent individuals driven by anti-white hatred. The criminalisation of Third World protest has a long and respectable history. One liberal critic of imperialism wrote in 1919:

> The idea of Nationalism is one of the most generally misunderstood in the modern world. The Imperialists do not even try to understand it: they simply call it sedition and hand it over to the police.[14]

This criminalisation of dissent required that the target be portrayed as a subversive rather then as a legitimate representative of national aspirations. Psychological warfare was the appropriate response to this challenge.

One of the first attempts to mount a sociological critique of the demonisation of anti-colonial nationalism was an article by S.K. Ratcliffe, published in 1908 in the British journal *The Sociological Review*. Ratcliffe noted the tendency to dismiss the national aspirations of India. 'It is ordinarily said, especially in England, that the Indian agitator and newspaper represent nobody but themselves.' Ratcliffe, who dismissed this patronising view, pointed to some of the arguments used to marginalise the Indian nationalist: 'we exaggerate the natural divisions of India: we exaggerate enormously the difference of race, of speech, and of creed; we misread, I am persuaded, the moral of Indian history before our own beneficent advent.'[15]

Ratcliffe's contribution was important, for it indicated that the attack on Indian nationalism was not conducted merely at the level of argument. It involved the rewriting of Indian history and the practice of promoting the 'natural divisions' of the continent, that is the policy of divide and rule. In other words, imperial intervention sought to weaken popular movements mobilised on a national basis by strengthening other more parochial foci of loyalty. In this way, any manifestation of regional or communal or religious loyalties could be used to substantiate the anti-nationalist thesis.

The assault on the legitimacy of Third World nationalism was also conducted on the moral plane. Western experts questioned the ability of the African or Asian to cope with the demands of modernity. And since nationalism was an expression of modernity, whatever anti-colonial politics was about it had little to do with genuine nationalism. Accordingly it was now proposed that Third World nationalism was not so much a symptom of modernity as a reaction to it. Resistance to the West was described as a 'clash of culture' – by implication a revolt against modernity. Anglo-American sociological literature during the interwar period helped in reinterpreting anti-colonial protest as a mani- festation of backward-looking impulses. An article published in 1927 in the *American Journal of Sociology*, 'The Social Background of Asiatic Nationalism', clearly expresses this approach:

> The ultimate source of much Asiatic nationalism is the individual's resistance to a change in habit patterns ... they had not been fitted for the new type of social order introduced by the West. An intel- lectual training had been provided which enabled them to understand Western ideas, but not the character formation which enabled them to function adequately in a dynamic competitive society.[16]

From this standpoint, Asiatic nationalism expressed a failure to cope – a defect of character rather then a legitimate quest for autonomy.

For the West, especially the imperial powers, contesting the legitimacy of anti-colonial nationalism was central to the maintenance of its power and authority. Anti-colonial aspirations directly called into question the right of the West to control the affairs of the world. At the ideologi- cal level, the issue of Western superiority was put to question. Most important of all, if the claims of anti-colonial movements were intrin- sically legitimate, then clearly Western imperialism was essentially unsupportable. In this sense the claims of anti-colonial nationalism challenged important tenets of the existing Western political culture. And they did so precisely at a time when imperial culture itself was becoming problematic. By the 1930s it was evident that the culture of imperialism was now on the defensive. In contrast to the past, the term imperialism itself had acquired a negative connotation among the public in Britain and the United States.

In Britain, steps were taken to improve the image of Empire. In March 1939 the Colonial Office established a Social Services Department and a year later it set up a Public Relations Department. More than ever, imperialism had to be marketed and sold. As we shall see in subsequent chapters, the imperial publicist found the task of combatting anti- colonial nationalism far from easy. It was easier to denigrate and discredit opponents than to put forward a positive case for Britain. At least unconsciously, the conclusion was drawn that while the Empire was beyond repair it was still possible to deprive anti-imperial opponents of moral legitimacy. In this way the damage caused by the decline of the Empire could be minimised.

Is it Nationalism?

It should be evident that the controversies which surround the question of nationalism are never merely academic in character. The affirmation of nationhood is at once a quest for authority and a claim to legitimacy. Opposition to this claim represents denial of its legitimacy. Every debate about the nationalist qualities of a specific movement represents competing claims to authority and ultimately to power. That is why virtually every assertion of anti-colonial nationalism has been contested by the West. What the Mau Mau movement of Kenya and the Nasser movement of Egypt have in common is that their claim to represent the aspiration of genuine nationalism was questioned by the West. Whenever the character of nationalism is made into an issue, it is a prologue to an assault on its authenticity.

Academic investigations of nationalism profess objectivity and detachment. To be sure, academic discussions of nationalism are invariably abstract and unable to yield to experience. By transforming nationalism into a distinct topic it is torn out of its historically determined context. Such a discussion implies that it is not history which throws up a nationalist response, but nationalism which makes history. It is as if this phenomenon has some inner dynamic of its own which drives it from one place to the next. Thus the British sociologist Maurice Ginsberg could write of the 'new areas to which nationalism is now spreading'. Others classify its different manifestations and draw contrasts between the nationalisms of which they approve and those of which they do not. So Hannah Arendt could contrast the liberal universalist nationalism to 'frustrated nationalism' and 'tribal nationalism'.[17]

The discussion on nationalism often confuses symptom and cause. Whether a movement is genuinely nationalist or not depends on the broader social forces that prevail. The balance of forces in society and the strength of competing claims are decisive in transforming the claims of individual nationalists into a mass nationwide movement.[18] As the recent experience of post-Stalinist societies shows, the success or failure of a specific nationalism does not depend on its inner strength, but on the influence of the wider environment in which it exists. The relatively successful emergence of Slovenia, for example, was not due the intensity of its nationalist sentiment but to its access to economic resources and

patrons in the West. Whether or not you certify a particular nationalism as 'genuine' invariably represents a political choice.

The issues that drive a nationalist movement may also be expressed
in a different form. Poverty, land hunger or a reaction to foreign
domination may well be expressed through religious outbursts or class
conflict. But none of these forms enjoys the international respectabil-
ity associated with nationalism. There are two fundamental reasons why
the national form tends to be adopted by movements. First the claim
to nationhood at least formally resolves the tension between particular
and society-wide interests. It is a claim made on behalf of the whole
community, and as such it provides a means for the leadership of a
movement to unite disparate forces. Secondly, the claim to nationalism is the internationally accepted road to exercising authority.

In the examination of any movement the crucial questions to ask are
to do with the social dynamic and the tensions it contains rather than
whether or not it meets the abstract criteria of nationalism. Nationalism means different things in different circumstances. It is a political idiom
through which a variety of conflicting motives can be expressed. The
exploration of social context and social determination provides the
necessary insights into the meaning of a particular nationalism.

Since the discussion of nationalism involves recognition or non-
recognition, it tends to have direct political consequences. It is a
discussion which can not remain untouched by the contest between
Western imperialists and anti-colonial forces. This influence is reflected
in the academic literature on European empires and decolonisation.
Scholars in this field tend to minimise the role of nationalist forces in
the shaping of events. American writers reach this conclusion through
questioning the indigenous character of anti-colonial revolts. As Gurtov
argued, the raising of the spectre of Soviet influence denied 'indigenous
roots, hence also the legitimacy, of radical movements'.[19]

British authors adopted a different strategy. In British imperial his-
toriography the main emphasis was to minimise the role of anti-imperialist
protest in the process of decolonisation. What emerged from this
literature was the self-flattering vision of an imperial power almost voluntarily preparing its subjects for eventual nationhood. According to
one recently published account the only nationalist force that Britain
ever had to face was in India and even that movement was 'founded
by – an Englishman'![20] The identical theme was constantly advanced
in the interwar period. 'It is enough to say that, if India is indeed a nation
now, as they claim it to be, then it is British work, British brains, British
energy and character, most of all British example and British inspira-

tion that have made it so', summed up this attitude.[21] It seems that even the launching of an anti-imperialist nationalist movement required British initiative. This point is ceaselessly repeated in texts on the subject. The stress on nationalism as a European export to the colonies has the effect of further diminishing the significance of anti-imperialist initiative. But this self-conscious repetition of the absence of an indigenous anti-colonial nationalist tradition also serves to expose the continuing Western anxieties regarding the subject of Third World nationalism.

The line between imperial propaganda and academic contributions to this subject is often unclear. The presentation of anti-colonial protest as the irrational outburst of malevolent forces is often reproduced in a more 'neutral' form in the academic literature. Take the example of the 1931 revolt against the British in Burma. The British Government and media systematically emphasised what they considered to be the exotic, primitive and irrational character of the rebels. The report of the Burma Government remarked that the 'Burman peasantry are incredibly ignorant and superstitious, the belief in the efficacy of charms and tattooing as conferring invulnerability being still widespread'. One Burmese politician, U Saw, was so incensed by this representation of events that he wrote a pamphlet, in which he reminded the British that 'the people of the most enlightened countries such as Russia, England, Scotland, Italy etc., are not free from old beliefs and superstitions'.[22] U Saw's argument found little resonance in the West.

J.S. Furnivall's well-known study of Burmese society illustrates the academic input to the discussion. In one sense Furnivall's *Colonial Policy and Practice* appears as a balanced contribution. It criticises the failures of British colonial policy in Burma. It is even prepared to accept the existence of nationalist sentiment with the qualification that 'nationalism of the modern type was a late development in Burma', thought 'not for lack of national sentiment but from ignorance of the modern world'. However, when Furnivall comes to examine specifics, in this case the 1931 uprising, the nationalist causation is systematically denied. He notes that it had only a 'very remote connection with modern nationalism' and added that it 'showed how little progress modern Nationalism had made among the people'. Furnivall's verdict was that the revolt was not nationalist but 'anti-Government and anti-European'.[23]

Furnivall's book was written at the request of the Governor of Burma in 1942 to assist the task of post-war reconstruction. It is therefore not surprising that he was inclined to accept the imperial version of events.

However, what is interesting is that other scholars without any imperial affiliations tended to interpret colonial developments from a similar standpoint. By the 1950s the imperial view of Third World nationalism dominated the Anglo-American literature on this subject. Any manifestation of anti-imperialist nationalist sentiment was subjected to intense scrutiny. The verdict was invariably that the movement was in some sense deeply flawed.

The strength of anti-nationalist academic opinion is revealed by the hesitant defensiveness of those few scholars who went against the stream. One of the first British academic texts sympathetic to the cause of African nationalism, Thomas Hodgkin's *Nationalism in Colonial Africa*, published in 1956, is self-consciously hesitant. Hodgkin is clearly aware that the nationalist claims of African movements were subject to question by his colleagues. In anticipation of such criticism, he wrote:

> But it is not a peculiarly African that, during a period of struggle for independence from foreign rule, the shape of the nations-to-be should remain somewhat cloudy and undefined, or that various competing or coexisting nationalisms, appealing to wider or narrower loyalties, should be thrown up in the process.[24]

Hodgkin was right to point to European precedents, for example the co-existence of Macedonian, Greater Bulgarian and Pan Slavic sentiments in the Balkans. In so doing he hinted at the double standard that Western writers applied to the study of nationalism in the colonial world.

The influence of the imperial interpretation of events on the specialist literature is palpable. This outcome was a consequence of an ideological battle which the West was determined to win. That the question 'is it nationalist?' was and continues to be posed so often suggests that the legitimate claims of anti-imperialist movements are still far from universally recognised.

The Problem of Imperial Identity

The peculiar intensity of the Western response to anti-colonial protest was motivated not merely by the fear of losing global power. This response was also shaped by the anxieties experienced at the level of imperial self-esteem. Today it is difficult to recall the centrality of imperialism to the identity of the turn of the century American and British elites. The assumptions of racial superiority and of imperial power influenced every aspect of the outlook of these elites. At this time the term imperialism was perceived in positive terms – it expressed the sentiment of adventure of a race born to rule.

When Lord Rosebery gave his Rector's address to Glasgow University in 1900 he predictably titled his lecture 'Questions of Empire'. He recalled how, 50 years before, 'the world looked lazily on while we discovered, developed, and annexed the waste or savage territories of the world'. He noted that the survival of the Empire required an 'imperial race – a race vigorous and industrious and intrepid' and exhorted the assembled educators to contribute to the rejuvenation of this race. Rosebery concluded that 'on that, under Providence, depends the future, and the immediate future, of the race; and what is empire but the predominance of race?'.[25]

The link between Empire and racial superiority was a comfortable reminder of distinction which reinforced the pride of the Anglo-American elite. It was a central component of the self-image of the imperialist mind. Yet by the 1920s it was being called into question by anti-colonial protest. The demand for national freedom was antithetical to the imperial sense of 'predominance of race'. The very recognition of claims to self-determination under the terms of the Treaty of Versailles invalidated important aspects of a hitherto unproblematic imperialist identity. It is not surprising that no sooner did President Woodrow Wilson affirm the principle of self-determination before doubts about it were raised by imperialist politicians. Robert Lansing, the Secretary of State to Wilson, recalled his doubts during the proceedings of the Peace Conference:

> The more I think about the Presidents declaration as to the right of 'self-determination', the more convinced I am of the danger of putting such ideas into the minds of certain races. It is bound to be basis of impossible demands on the Peace Conference and create trouble in many lands.
>
> What effect will it have on the Irish, the Indians, the Egyptians, and the nationalists among the Boers? Will it not breed discontent, disorder and rebellion? Will not the Mohammedans of Syria and Palestine and possibly of Morocco and Tripoli rely on it?[26]

For Lansing and his class it was unthinkable that all races could possess the right to nationhood. What was at stake was that sense of superiority which was so vital to imperial self-confidence.

There were, of course, many factors that contributed to the crisis of imperial self-confidence. Imperialist rivalries which led to the slaughter of the First World War destroyed once and for all the myth of a civilising mission. The Russian Revolution of 1917 and upheavals throughout the world indicated that there was no return to the pre-war era of uncontested Western domination. Even within the metropolitan environment, defenders of Empire were on the defensive. Increasingly imperialism acquired a negative connotation in the public mind. It was symptomatic of the mood of the interwar years that many advocates of Empire took care no longer to refer to themselves as imperialist.

Anti-colonial nationalism helped to strengthen the crisis of imperial legitimacy. It also struck a blow at imperial self-esteem. Anti-colonial movements not only claimed independence from the West – by their very existence they questioned the assumption of superiority. The Anglo-American elite could not accept such claims without undermining its own moral and intellectual standing. However, times had changed and it was no longer possible to celebrate the imperialist mission and the virtues of race.

Forced into an ideological corner, imperialist publicists and thinkers could not offer a positive account of themselves. But they could retain a degree of credibility by demolishing their opponents. This was the peculiar context in which the demonisation of Third World movements became a central feature of imperialist political culture before and after the Second World War. In the new international climate of anti-imperialism, advocates of Empire were forced on to the retreat. But they could limit the damage by discrediting their opponents. How and why and with what consequences is the subject of the chapters that follow.

2 A Presentiment of Danger: the Preoccupation with White Prestige

The Western tendency to query the authenticity of anti-colonial nationalism was preceded by a phase of anxious anticipation. Anti-colonial nationalism was nervously expected some time before it actually emerged as a coherent force. Throughout the interwar period alarmist reports tended, if anything, to invent or at least to exaggerate the peril from Africa and Asia. In both the popular press and the more specialist accounts writers warned of the dangers of the different PAN movements. Pan-Africanism, Pan-Arabism, Pan-Islam or Pan-Asianism were all at one time or another represented as potentially explosive forces. Since such movements had little real strength at the time, these panicky reactions above all betrayed the crisis of confidence within the imperialist culture of the West.

The characteristic feature of the Western response to the colonial world during these years was to anticipate dangers that were imminent but still unclear. This reaction is well illustrated in Louis Snyder's *Race: A History of Modern Ethnic Theories*. Published in 1939, and written from the standpoint of American liberalism, it was a pioneering critique of racist politics. Snyder was deeply troubled by the reaction that Western racism was likely to provoke among people of colour. 'It is as yet too early to know the form in which pan-Africanism will be consolidated', he stated. Despite these doubts about exactly what Pan-Africanism would be, however, Snyder was certain that it would become a formidable force. 'It appears certain', he wrote, that the 'movement will one day progress beyond its present stage'. Typically for his time, Snyder does not expand on this point. The premise for his certainty is left to the imagination of the reader.

The same lack of focus is also evident in Snyder's speculation of impending dangers from Asia:

Pan-Asianism has not yet crystallized into an active and competing force. Still somewhat vague and intangible in concept, there is no doubt that it will one day be grounded solidly in the mass mind of Asiatics through propagandistic methods learned from the West.[1]

It is curious that he had 'no doubt' that something which was as yet unformed would become a formidable force in the future. His stress on the future threat of anti-Western nationalism expressed the mood of the time. The literature on nationalism and international relations, published on both sides of the Atlantic, conveyed many such indefinite apprehensions.

The adjectives used to describe the peril of nationalism were extravagant and even sensationalist. Yet discussion about the problem of these as yet unformed nationalisms is singularly uninformative concerning the nature of the challenge facing the West. It is important to emphasise this point: *the reaction of almost panic-like proportions actually precedes the emergence of mass anti-imperialist movements!*

The lack of serious consideration of what constituted the problem of nationalism suggests that the conviction of imminent danger was more the product of a social mood in the West than a response to a direct menace in the colonial world. The one milestone which authors pointed to as a major influence on the discussion of nationalism was the experience of the First World War. According to many accounts, this war undermined the reputation of Western civilisation and eroded what is often described as 'white prestige'. In the 1920s and 1930s the Great War was often portrayed by popular and specialist writers alike as a symbol of Western weakness and decline.

Accounts of the impact of the First World War on the colonial world published during the interwar years were highly evocative and even alarmist. Some feared that as a result of serving in the war, colonial soldiers had seen through the 'white man' and would therefore soon demand a different relationship with their imperial masters. The liberal missionary Basil Matthews warned that demobilised Indian soldiers were bringing nationalist politics to the villages. According to Matthews, they 'linked up village India with world-wide movements and in particular with the wave of nationalistic self-determination'. Even more disturbing for Matthews was the suspicion that Indian nationalists had 'conceived a contempt' for 'white civilization'.[2] It was this fear of both rebellion and rejection which underscored the Western presentiment of danger. It was as if all the claims and pretensions of the West were now under critical scrutiny. That conclusion was accepted by many of the contributors to a conference of American academics on the subject of *Public Opinion and World Peace* in December 1921. The consensus was that the war had let the cat out of the bag. 'It laid bare the skeleton in the closet of western civilization' was the view of one contributor, who added that even 'the most backward of these countries is now alive to the spirit of renewed nationalism that is sweeping the world'.[3] The British socialist academic Harold Laski was no less sensitive than committed imperialists to the danger represented by this spirit. He told his audience in 1932 that 'I do not myself see how the effort of Asia to win its independence can easily be attained without at least the prospect of grave disaster to the world'. And he added: 'Today it is Asia; will it be Africa to-morrow?'[4]

Despite the emphatic character of warnings of nationalisms that were 'sweeping the world' and threatening 'grave disaster', the quality of discussion was incoherent and superficial. Allusions to the Balkans or the growth of nationalist sentiment in Europe acted as substitutes for investigating developments in the colonial world. There was little attempt to analyse and disclose the dynamic at work in Africa or Asia.

To take the example of the growing concern with the rise of African nationalism in the American and British literature: African nationalism was seldom the main or explicit subject of the discussion. Descriptions and comments on African nationalism were incidental to the main subject under consideration. These coded references emphasised the theme of retribution and revenge. Authors warned against the practice of crude colonial domination in order to contain the passion of revenge. Diedrich Westermann, a key figure in the London-based International Institute of African Languages and Culture noted that an 'undue sense of superiority, of exaggerated racial pride, and of physical aversion towards the Natives may develop, possibly also of hate and fear when Natives begin to compete with the white man in certain spheres of work'.[5]

Because the subject was so closely intertwined with the history of Western domination, colonial nationalism was perceived as a direct challenge to the *status-quo*. The discussion thus inevitably took on the character of a warning to the West. Nationalism was not a subject for detached scholars. The literature was really devoted to exploring not nationalism as such but the perceived *danger* it represented. Virtually every contribution alluded to this danger that would arrive in the not too distant future. Articles on this subject in the *American Journal of Sociology* were distinctly downbeat on this point. One author, writing in 1935, remarked that as the South African 'native absorbs European culture he will attempt to penetrate the European world ... and that out of the conflict born of this penetration, race consciousness will emerge' and 'growing sophistication will give a knowledge of European national-ism'.[6]

The contribution of British social anthropologists contains a veritable harvest of hints warning of the none too distant arrival of African nationalism. Malinowski was categorical on this point. He pointed to what he saw as 'the new African type of nationalism' of 'racial feeling, and of collective opposition to western culture' which he argued was 'of the greatest importance'.[7] Ironically, although it was 'of the greatest importance', Malinowski did not dwell on the subject. The pointed reference and the strongly worded aside were the procedures that authors adopted in their consideration of African nationalism. This fashion continued well into the 1940s. Even as late as 1952 a key American text on race relations could speculate as follows:

> How many peoples there will be in Africa in the future, no one can say. But it is safe to say that there will be politically active groups with a strong sense of mission to free the dark peoples from domination by the white. What will be their language (since there is no candidate for a national literary language), their territorial limits, their philosophy; who their leaders – these things no one can say.[8]

Such speculations manifest a very real sense of foreboding. The pattern that emerges is of a discourse which is elliptic and ambivalent about its subject matter. Although the discussion of nationalism was invariably conducted in the future tense, it provides evidence of already existing insecurities. The failure to elaborate the subject indicates a lack of openness or at least a reluctance to confront the subject head on. It is tempting to draw the conclusion that the authors practised a form of self-censorship on the ground that explicitness would only encourage that which they feared. There was at work a self-consciousness which feared that too open a discussion would only reveal the weaknesses of the West and thereby accelerate the rise of forces beyond anyone's control.

The Western discussion of anti-imperialist nationalism featured anxiety-ridden reactions about the dangers ahead. At the same time, however, the discussion was constrained by inhibitions about openly considering the consequences of anti-Western sentiments. To illustrate the working out of these tensions it is useful to look at the delibera-tions of the British elite on the subject of the demobilised colonial soldier during the Second World War. In particular, the debate about demo-bilised colonial soldiers can show how Western authorities transferred their own fears about the future of imperialism on to the notion of a threat from the colonies. An examination of this story may reveal, too, that the insecurities evident in imperial reactions during the 1940s are not unconnected to the aggressive anti-Third World sentiments of today.

The Demobilised Soldier and the Blow to White Prestige

The object of this detour is to explore the sense of fear that surrounded the imperial discussion during the Second World War of the likely consequences of the demobilisation of colonial troops. The aim here is not so much an analysis of what actually happened but of what British and other Western officials feared would happen. Any historian investigating official correspondence for the period will be struck by the discrepancy between the prevalence of imperial concern and the relative absence of specific causes of this concern. It was as if the sheer weight of the reaction made it unnecessary to elaborate the problem. No one seemed to ask why returning colonial troops should constitute such a grave problem.

It seems probable that the imperial panic or overreaction regarding demobilisation has influenced much of the subsequent academic discussion on the subject. The significance attached to the role of returning colonial soldiers was uncritically accepted by the subsequent specialist literature, especially by Africanists. They suggested that participation in the war had a transformative effect on the consciousness of African soldiers. The generation of scholars who followed routinely accepted this standpoint as an article of faith. Writing in this vein, Ali Mazrui has argued that to 'witness a white man scared to death under fire was itself a revelation to many Africans, who had previously seen white men only in their arrogant commanding positions as a colonial elite'.[9] Soldiers who experienced the trial of warfare alongside Europeans would no longer tolerate colonial domination, was the conclusion drawn by most writers on the subject. Not infrequently they were accorded a pivotal role in anti-colonial nationalism.

The link between soldiers and the coming of nationalism has been challenged by Rita Headrick, who argues that there is 'little evidence for the political awakening' of African soldiers and by David Killingray whose discussion of ex-servicemen on the Gold Coast suggests that the majority of these veterans were 'bystanders to nationalist politics'.[10] These writers provide a useful antidote to the conventional wisdom regarding the centrality of returning soldiers. However, our concern is not to take sides in this debate but to consider the curious phenomenon of imperialist panic.

There is a clear link between the writing on this subject in the 1940s and 1950s and the imperial view. Most of the early writers who attached great significance to the political role of demobilised soldiers based their views directly on those of imperial officials.[11] Whitehall mandarins of all shades of opinion were convinced that when colonial soldiers demobilised they would constitute a major challenge to the Empire. Throughout the conduct of the war, direct statements and frequent remarks indicated intense nervousness about the danger posed by returning soldiers. Specialists at the Ministry of Information were convinced that this danger could not be avoided. At best its negative effects could be curbed. This was the view taken by the Ministry's 1944 *Plan of Propaganda to British West Africa*. The authors of the plan predicted that demobilised soldiers would not willingly return to the land – 'discontent will almost inevitably ensue unless the prospects of farm life can be rendered reasonably attractive'.[12] This view, firmly held by those involved with planning for postwar reconstruction – continued to influence the British Colonial Office into the 1950s. The sentiment was clearly expressed by the former Secretary of State for the Colonies, Arthur Creech-Jones when he linked the process of decolonisation as in part a response to the political pressure of the demobilised:

> The experience which came to tens of thousands of colonial soldiers in the war years released influences and stimulated ideas which were incalculable. They became racially aware of themselves; new political notions dawned or spread among people who had previously been conscious only of kinship and tribal association.[13]

By this time, Creech-Jones's assessment of the central role of the returning soldier was accepted by his colleagues and by specialists as being above controversy. The very absence of substantiation for this view raises interesting questions as to how this conclusion was arrived at.

An Unspecified Threat

Creech-Jones's retrospective account of the role of colonial soldiers was based on well-established knowledge of the British imperial establishment. Certain points did not need to be spelled out. Colonial soldiers who travelled afar were thought to be vulnerable to insidious influences. That demobilised soldiers would constitute a threat was assumed to be a fact of life at all levels of officialdom, though the nature of the problem was rarely explored. This was an unspecified danger, though those dealing with running the Empire had no doubt about what was at stake. But what strikes the historian are the omissions in the discussion. It is as if it was sufficient to use the word 'demobilisation' to convey clear meaning: the official mind preferred to deal with this problem through a series of coded allusions, as if the very act of making the danger explicit made matters worse.

Concern about the problem of the returning soldier was presented in public in a relatively restrained form. Naturally, wartime imperial propaganda ignored the problem altogether and tried to play up the loyalty of the great martial races of the Empire. But somehow the message of this propaganda sounded more perfunctory than before. Imperial administrators clearly liked soldiers drawn from those whom they considered to be martial races. Some still believed that colonial troops provided the cornerstone for local loyalty. For example Sir Philip Mitchell, Governor of Fiji, proposed in 1943 that Fijians, Tongans and Solomon Islanders should be given the opportunity of forming a garrison in the Pacific. 'It has all sorts of prestige and moral values, about which I need not enlarge, as experience in Africa shows', wrote Mitchell.[14] Celebration of loyal colonial martial races coexisted with fearing the worst about demobilisation. But then recruitment during the Second World War went beyond the traditional pool of recruits, and British officials had no means of verifying the degree of loyalty of new recruits.

The British government and its postwar planners took a keen interest in the issue of demobilisation. In July 1942 a circular despatch was issued on the subject and a committee was established in London to deal with the problem. By the end of the war machinery had been established in every British colony to deal with the problem of demobilisation. For its part the Ministry of Information was experimenting with developing propaganda that would be most effective in dealing with the grievances of demobilised soldiers.[15] That these were more than paper initiatives was confirmed by the Secretary of State for the Colonies, Stanley Oliver, in November 1943: 'On my recent visit to Africa I was much struck by the interest which is taken everywhere in the problems of demobilisation and post war settlement', wrote Oliver to Sir William Jowitt, the Head of the Committee on Demobilisation.[16]

Oliver was probably referring to the widespread official initiatives taken by local administrators to establish a machinery to cater for the returning soldier.[17] But at the same time, conversation among European officials often revealed deep anxieties regarding the threat posed by the demobilised veterans. 'God, so that's what we've got coming to us after the War', was the reaction of some Europeans watching a display of close combat by African troops in Northern Rhodesia in the spring of 1943.

Dire predictions of dangers to come were an integral part of casual conversation among Europeans in Africa.[18] Reports by Captain A.G. Dickson, head of a mobile propaganda unit in East Africa, confirm the widespread nature of these reactions. In a report on Uganda, Dickson noted that after Special Services troops dealt with a prison riot in Lugazi it was an 'open joke among' the European officers at Kampala 'that their real "blooding" would have to wait till the Uganda troops returned home on demobilisation'. Dickson continued:

> Not one but almost every District Commissioner espoused anxiety regarding the return of troops – not on any score of the difficulty of economic reabsorption, but the expectation of 'trouble' in the Irish sense of the word and on a large scale. This was particularly the case in Acholi. This atmosphere of dread regarding the undisciplined African home from the wars dominated conversation. There was something unpleasantly sinister in the way Administrative Officers would frankly urge us to fire our weapons so that Africans might appreciate the futility of arguing with Bren guns.[19]

We shall return shortly to probe what Dickson meant by 'trouble in the Irish sense of the word', but for now it is sufficient to note the prevalence of this anxiety in official reports and correspondence.

Rita Headrick in her discussion of 'African Soldiers in World War II' notes that the 'returning soldier was awaited with some apprehension'. She remarks how 'almost all the reports on postwar planning' began with noting the transformation of African soldiers. Reports invariably began by citing how the experience of the war had changed the African soldier and raised his expectations. The phrase reiterated almost word for word in many accounts was that 'soldiers who have learned new skills and trades in the forces are not going to be content to go back to agricultural life'.[20] A major Cabinet memorandum calling for the extension of colonial development and welfare measures was prefaced with the same standard warning about the soldiers who 'will return with a desire for some of the improved conditions which they have seen and experienced elsewhere'.[21]

Standard phrases about the opportunities that the new skills of demobilised soldiers provided for colonial development barely concealed deep-rooted anxieties regarding the future. The unknown postwar order and the soon-to-return veteran were treated interchangeably in the imagination of officials and postwar planners. From this perspective, broader concerns regarding imperial control were most clearly symbolised by the returning soldier. By 1943 the notion that demo-

bilisation would lead to discontent was uncontested by the administrators of the British Empire. The main protagonist in contemporary
imperial accounts was the returning African soldier, the personification
of all the dangers confronting colonial order.

Officials in Whitehall were consciously preparing senior administrators in the colonies for the problem of handling the threat posed by
demobilised soldiers. The fear of disturbances motivated the delibera-
tions of the Ministry of Information regarding demobilisation in the
colonies. This was a theme which informed the different propaganda
plans drawn up for the various colonies. *A Plan of Propaganda to British
West Africa* outlined the problem in the following way:

> Since the war thousands of West Africans serving in the forces have
> acquired higher standards of diet and hygiene, and have been trained
> in some trade or vocation involving in many cases a considerable degree
> of mechanical skill. Those who have been in foreign service have in
> addition been educated by contact with other nationalities. Most of
> this educational work has been undertaken for reasons of military
> necessity, and its long term results cannot as yet be assessed, but
> discontent will almost inevitably be aroused if the demobilised troops
> are obliged to return to a primitive life.[22]

The view that discontent would arise 'almost inevitably' was shared by
officials on the ground. The American Consul in Accra reported that
the 'Gold Coast Government is anticipating with some trepidation the
return from the Far East of the thousands of its men now serving in the
armed forces and is taking steps to minimize the dislocation which is
bound to occur.'[23]

The language used by correspondents to describe the problem conveys
the impression that trouble was unavoidable – 'bound to occur', to use
the words of the American Consul, or 'inevitable', in the case of the
Whitehall propaganda plan for West Africa. An editorial in *The Times*
also had the character of a warning: 'the return of these men in their
thousands – without their officers – may well jeopardise the whole fabric
of indirect rule'.[24] The equation of trouble with the returning soldier
was firmly established in the imperial mind.

As the end of the war approached the anxieties became more
pronounced. Increasingly, it appeared that the fears expressed on the
subject of the returning soldier were about to be confirmed. In his
statement regarding the 1945 disturbances in Uganda, the Governor
did not fail to point to the impending return of soldiers and the 'shock
to the social and economic order which the return of demobilised soldiers

may produce'.[25] At a stroke the future problem of returning soldiers
became linked to the already existing conflict that was shaking Uganda.

The connections drawn by the Uganda administration between
demobilising soldiers and the problem of maintaining order in Buganda
were at best indirect:

> it must also be remembered that we are this year receiving back 15000
> soldiers who enlisted from Buganda. This return cannot fail to have
> certain repercussions on the social, economic and political structures
> of the tribe, and it is necessary to avoid any act which would
> complicate the already difficult task of ensuring their peaceful reab-
> sorption into civil life.[26]

The returning *askari* had become a source of apprehension, a challenge
to postwar stability. It was as if the demobilised soldier provided a focus
through which a sense of declining imperial power could be understood.
The fears expressed about the returning *askari* were vague, but the
underlying anxiety was highly concentrated. The warning issued by the
Headquarters of East Africa Command in 1946 were typically indeter-
minate: 'the possibility of disturbances occurring, now that most of the
troops have been demobilised, will increase'.[27] In London, too, anxieties
regarding the Empire were expressed in relation to the returning soldier.

The demobilised soldier also figured prominently in the deliberations
that surrounded the discussion of postwar security. British Governors
of East Africa at their conference in June 1945 anticipated a major
escalation of political activity and undertook to establish an 'efficient
political security organisation'. Military planners were particularly
concerned to establish contingency plans to deal with unrest in the future.
The most interesting aspect of the plans is the sense of malaise and doubt
that they reveal. A report on Kenya speculates that 'unrest is also
possible as a direct result of demobilisation'. Lack of economic opportunities are presented as the potential cause of future conflict. 'It must
be borne in mind that while serving in the forces these men have learned
the value of co-operation', the report warns. While these warnings of
unrest due to economic grievances appear relatively rational, the plans
drawn up for Zanzibar reveal a panic-like fear of the future:

> Unrest in Zanzibar might come to a head with little warning,
> following underground preparation. Mobs might be armed with
> swords and spears: and possibly a few shotguns and be led by ex-
> servicemen with a slight knowledge of leadership.[28]

The projection of such fantastic scenarios was not thought to be over-reactive. The expectation of disorder was widespread throughout the colonies. That it would come seemed beyond dispute – the only subject of debate was the form that conflict would take.

The discrepancy between the fears expressed regarding the returning colonial soldier and the actual record of unrest is striking. There were of course disturbances and even small-scale mutinies of local troops in Africa. But overall imperial control was rarely challenged and even less frequently threatened by colonial soldiers. Clearly there was a great divergence between imperial perception and events on the ground.

The fact that fears about the returning soldier even predated the outbreak of the Second World War suggests that these anxieties had little to do with real events on the ground. Similar reactions were evident before, during and after the First World War, and concerns about sending African troops overseas were aired in the late 1930s. So what were the influences that disposed imperial officials to adopt such an insecure tone in their discussion of demobilisation in the colonies?

Problem of Control

The fears articulated about the returning colonial soldier were in fact an expression of an acute imperial sensitivity towards the problem of control. The experience of the Second World War, especially after the British setbacks in Asia, intensified imperial insecurities. Many of these fears were to be experienced in a racial form. Japan's successes against the British in Malaya and Burma were interpreted as setbacks to what was called 'white prestige'. Officials feared that colonial troops would at once see the weakness of imperial control and the decline of white prestige. As indicated previously, such reactions were not new. What was different this time was the international climate as regards racial issues. White superiority was no longer seen as unproblematic even by the most strident advocates of Empire. Issues of control, loyalty and white prestige had seemed to merge in the imperial imagination.

The fear of losing control often led to an exaggerated appreciation of the problems. When, in February 1942, some soldiers of the 25th East Africa Brigade refused to embark for overseas service on the grounds that they had no home leave for two years, the overreaction at Whitehall was palpable. Anger was particularly directed at General Platt for accepting this *fait accompli* and allowing the men to go on leave. 'This is indeed a tragedy', minuted one official, who added that 'news will fly around East Africa and African morale, both military and civilian will be badly shaken'.[29] The dread of imperial weakness informed the reaction in London. In fact Platt's entirely sensible decision had no political repercussions in East Africa.

That questions would arise about the loyalty of colonial troops was inevitable. Here was a group of organised soldiers who had some considerable power in the colonial context. As one editorial writer in South Africa noted, 'the unspoken fear has always been – "Won't they turn the guns on us?"'.[30] 'They' were, of course, black and 'us' were white. After the ease with which Japan conquered the European colonies of Asia, the question of loyalty became increasingly indistinguishable from considerations of race. There was some concern that Japan's message of anti-white racial solidarity would find some resonance among colonial troops. There was also a growing awareness that relations between white and non-white were changing. According to reports, colonial troops were becoming 'colour conscious'.

Reports suggested that colonial troops were increasingly angered by the various manifestations of racial discrimination.[31] Race had become an issue and London could not remain indifferent to the sensitivity of colonial troops. So when the War Office offered the use of the Caribbean regiment for deployment in Asia, it warned the Commander in Chief in India that 'the men are extremely colour conscious and expect to be treated as white troops'.[32]

The need to minimise 'colour consciousness' was motivated by the presentiment that as white prestige declined so there would emerge a revolt of the non-white. It was feared that colonial troops would develop loyalties along lines of colour. This was the wartime version of the interwar panics over Pan-Asianism or Pan-Africanism. That is why Whitehall was concerned that colonial troops would be 'contaminated' with unacceptable ideas by black American troops. It was feared that black American soldiers would subvert the existing racial balance in the Empire. 'I imagine that in an ideal world we should certainly wish to avoid having British African personnel serving alongside American coloured troops', wrote A.H. Poynton of the Colonial Office. The considerable body of correspondence on this subject indicated that Poynton was not alone. Administrators from different parts of the Empire were firmly against allowing their local soldiers to fight alongside black Americans. They were no less firm in their opposition to the stationing of black American soldiers in the colonies.[33]

But wartime was not an 'ideal world', and colonial subjects could not be sealed off from having contact with black American soldiers.

Governors complained and blamed instances of unrest on the influence of black American soldiers on the local population. Governor Clifford of Trinidad went straight to the point: 'though neither are wanted here, Puerto Ricans would be preferable to United States' negroes'.[34] The British War Office was sensitive to racial considerations, but the exigency of fighting the war forced it to compromise. While it accepted the view that 'neither West nor East Africans should serve in Europe', it could not guarantee that these troops could be isolated from black Americans.[35] The tension between racial anxieties and military pragmatism shaped the discussion on the deployment of colonial troops.

Remarkably the available correspondence was also rarely explicit on the subject of racial concerns. When the question of black American soldiers serving alongside colonial troops arose, the War Office alluded to impenetrable 'political considerations'. And when it did elaborate on the subject, the racial motif was rarely mentioned. It suggested the possibility of 'trouble' on 'account of wide differences of outlook and terms of service' between American and colonial troops.[36] But of course if this was the real issue, why was the objection far more muted when it came to the exposing of colonial soldiers to white American troops?

It is difficult to be certain as to whether this pathological sensitivity to the subject of race was due to the new climate which was rhetorically critical of discrimination or to an awareness that the open acknowledgement of the problem would be interpreted as a sign of weakness. No doubt both influences were at play. From the available evidence it seems that officials were inhibited from expressing their fears openly in case they inadvertently encouraged anti-Western racial solidarity and nationalism. Officials at Whitehall reacted strongly against any open discussion of the problem. As far as they were concerned such discussion could only make matters worse. Colonial Office mandarins objected to a report of the Demobilisation (Machinery) Committee which explicitly discussed the 'colour question'. However, once it was clear that the report was not designed for publication the Colonial Office withdrew its dissent.[37] A kind of silent discourse of omissions and allusions was the acceptable language for dealing with the issue of race. The unspecified fears regarding the threat of the demobilised soldier were complemented by an all too meaningful silence on racial concerns.

We can now return to consider what Captain Dickson meant when he noted that the widespread fear regarding the returning soldier was not due to the 'difficulty of economic reabsorption' but to the 'expecta-

tion of "trouble" in the Irish sense of the word and on a large scale'.
The trouble that he referred to was, of course, political revolt motivated
by some form of anti-colonial impulse. This was the expectation of a
challenge to imperial control. But the most interesting part of Dickson's
statement was his dismissal of the problem of 'economic reabsorption',
since this observation went entirely against the grain of imperial pronouncements. Virtually every other statement on the subject dealt with
the problem of the economic integration of the returning veteran.
Western officials preferred to interpret the challenge to the *status-quo*
in economic rather than political terms. The imperial mind was much
more at ease with treating this problem as one susceptible to economic
solutions. The desire for economic advance did not, as such, threaten
Western authority. Unlike the Irish 'troubles' which fundamentally
challenged – and indeed continue to challenge – British authority,
economic demands could be contained relatively easily. That is why
the British felt so much more comfortable with an economic diagnosis
of the problem. Inner fears to do with race and control were represented in rational development terms.

From the available evidence, Dickson's statement emerges as an
astute appreciation of the situation. Four years later, the social anthropologist Raymond Firth, closely involved with Colonial Office research,
confirmed that the problem of the economic integration of demobilised
soldiers in West Africa was 'apparently, being solved with less difficulty
than was expected'.[38] In a sense the prominence given to the problem
of economic absorption was closely linked to the imperial overreaction to the consequences of demobilisation. The general fears regarding
imperial control and the racial sensibility through which they were experienced was expressed through the more neutral and technical language
of economics.

Economic demands did not touch on such fundamental questions as
sovereignty and imperialist authority. That was why the imperial
discourse was so ready to conflate political grievances and economic
ones. By prioritising economic issues over political ones, the imperial
mind sought to preserve the global status quo. This was a logic which
ran counter to the aspiration for autonomy. Hans Kohn observed in
the 1930s that 'it is the peculiarity and the delusion of the age of nationalism that national freedom is valued more highly than good government
or economic prosperity'.[39] This counterposition was actually quite
misplaced. For the colonial world, autonomy was perceived as the *precondition* for economic prosperity. Without autonomy, colonial economics

reduced itself to the propaganda exercises of Western development agencies.

The difficulty of openly expressing the apprehension of racial or anti-colonial revolt appeared to help consolidate the imperial overreaction to the demobilised soldier. The difficulty of directly and openly confronting the issue of race may well have led to the exaggerated appreciation of the problem. These tensions were reinforced by the realisation that, whatever the racial reservations of the imperial authorities, pragmatic considerations demanded the use of colonial troops. Non-white troops were needed for the conduct of the war effort. Racial reservations had to give way to the demands of the war. Consequently there could not be an open discussion of the subject.[40]

What Did They See?

Accounts of demobilised soldiers in official and specialist publications continually linked their experience abroad to the decline of white prestige. It was held that the experience of living with and fighting alongside Europeans changed the attitude of colonial subjects towards their masters. This fear of 'the destruction of white prestige as a result of military training' was noted in one of the early scholarly discussions of African ex-servicemen.[41] Headrick also remarked that 'Englishmen writing on the effects of the war on Africans exhibit an overriding concern for "the prestige of the white race", something usually assumed to have fallen'.[42] It is curious that the concept of white prestige has not become a subject of more serious investigation given its importance in the imperialist vocabulary.

Again, the accounts of what the colonial troops saw that would change their attitude are characteristically vague, as are the explanations for why this should lead to the fall of white prestige. However, the sheer volume of references to this process suggests that it was a deeply held reaction. It seems that the fears regarding the decline of white prestige were an expression of the crisis of confidence within the culture of imperialism itself. The identity of the Anglo-American elites, based on a strong sense of race and imperial mission, took a hard knock in the 1940s. White superiority, which represented a positive affirmation of Western identity, had become problematic. More than anything, the changing racial global balance seemed to symbolise imperial decline. From this standpoint the war, indeed both world wars could be interpreted as an indictment of the white race.

The impact of the war, the decline of white prestige and its discon-
certing consequences for imperial self-esteem were well expressed
retrospectively by the British Prime Minister Harold Macmillan in a
letter written to the Australian Prime Minister Robert Menzies in
1962. For Macmillan the changing relationship between white and non-
white people was disturbing. He reminded Menzies that they were 'born
into a very different world'. This different world was one where
European domination was unquestioned and 'where the civilised world
meant really Europe and its extensions overseas'.

Macmillan had no doubt about how this change had come about:

> what the two wars did was to destroy the prestige of the white
> people. For not only did the yellows and blacks watch them tear each
> other apart, committing the most frightful crimes and acts of barbarism
> against each other, but they actually saw them enlisting each their
> own yellows and blacks to fight other Europeans, other whites. It
> was bad enough for the white men to fight each other, but it was
> worse when they brought in their dependents.[43]

In Macmillan's eyes, the colonial soldier is represented as the eye-
witness to the white race at its worse. After this experience the traditional
relation of superior–inferior could no longer be sustained. It is as if white
prestige had been caught with its pants down. According to this scenario,
when he returns, the demobilised soldier will tell everyone about what
he saw. The problem of the demobilised soldier is at once the problem
of imperial legitimacy.

What was really at issue was not what the colonial soldier actually
saw, but what the imperial mind *feared* he had seen. Western imperialists had lost their confidence both in their project and in their ability
to maintain their global position. The emergence of Japan was one
symptom of the challenge to the West. But for a variety of reasons imperialists also found it difficult to believe in themselves. By the 1930s they
were both morally and intellectually on the defensive.[44] It was the deep-
seated crisis of self-belief which strengthened the expectation that
colonial soldiers would see through the whole charade. Whether they
did so or not was not the main issue.

Viewing the world through an already defensive outlook, imperialists automatically interpreted many actions of their colonial subjects as
proof of their own worst fears. Sensing their own weakness they
endowed the demobilised soldier with power and powerful insights.
They visited their own fears about the future on to the spectre of the
rebellious returning colonial soldier, who knew the dark secrets of his

white masters. And the sense of race which had helped to nourish the imperial identity was now an uncomfortable reminder of decline.

There are no significant examples of organised revolt by ex-colonial soldiers in Africa. Yet the demobilised veteran continued to be the focus of concern. For example, black American soldiers and returned veterans were blamed for the Maasina Rule protest movement in the Solomon Islands in 1947–8. Often local administrators who wanted to draw the attention of Whitehall would make pointed remarks about ex-soldiers. 'There were now some ten to fifteen thousand ex-servicemen in Jamaica and some might easily take to violence' argued a senior official in his pursuit of financial assistance from London.[45] That these ten to fifteen thousand Jamaicans were not organised, did not meet and did not necessarily have any collective existence did not matter, for the ex-servicemen had become one of those categories of the imperial imagination whose meaning was self-evident. Is it surprising that historians who have inspected the available documents often discover how the Second World War was 'the beginning of the end of the white man's prestige'?[46]

Despite the absence of any examples of racial revolt, serving colonial troops, too, continued to excite the imperial imagination. Sometimes even military pragmatism had to give way. Even in France, where the tradition of deploying colonial troops was far more established than in Britain, there was concern after the end of Second World War about being too reliant on them. According to Echenberg, De Gaulle insisted on the need for 'troops entirely French' to be stationed in the colonies. And this despite the fact that the French were relatively relaxed about the use of non-white troops. In contrast, South Africa's leaders were mentally preparing themselves for a race war. In their mind the process of decolonisation was synonymous with the 'arming of the native'. It was with this problem in mind that the nationalist leader D.F. Malan in 1945 suggested that the Western powers collaborate to demilitarise the continent and ensure that Africans were not 'given military training or be armed'.[47]

But the continuing preoccupation with race was not the monopoly of insecure white South Africans. Britain's Commonwealth Relations Secretary, Gordon Walker, feared the consequences of the growth of South African influence in East Africa. He warned that 'terrible wars might even be fought' between a 'white-ruled Eastern Africa and a black-ruled Western Africa'.[48] Such improbable scenarios continued the tradition of the racial panics that surrounded the issue of deploying colonial troops.

Conclusion

The anxieties expressed in the imperial perception of the problem of demobilisation suggest that what was really at issue was the moral crisis of British imperialism. Whatever the problems facing the Empire, the sense of moral malaise disposed officials towards overreaction. It was not difficult to overreact at a time when, after the experience of the fall of Singapore and Burma, the loyalty of colonial subjects was publicly questioned.

In a sense the apprehension and defensive orientation towards the issue of demobilisation suggests that whatever victorious posture the imperialists struck in public their inner sensibility was deeply disturbed. Underpinning the discussion of demobilisation was the clear suggestion that as far as the Empire was concerned the situation would get worse. Public pronouncements would continue to present the image of certainty and clarity of purpose. But an examination of imperial perceptions regarding demobilisation suggests that at least emotionally the British establishment had given up on the Empire. No doubt this sentiment helped undermine the outward determination to retain global influence through the Empire.

The reaction to demobilisation indicated that what was at stake during the war was not only the weakening of imperial control, but that this process was experienced by the imperial mind in an exaggerated form. The consequence of this reaction was no doubt to encourage the growth of precisely those forces that were feared. Having invented the militant demobilised soldier, Whitehall would soon face some real anti-colonial opponents.

The point here is, however, that the presentiment of danger — whether in the form of Third World nationalism, anti-Western racial solidarity or the revolt of colonial troops — *precedes* the emergence of the formidable challenge of anti-imperialist forces in the 1940s. Many of these panicky reactions were really a response to the erosion of the self-confidence of imperialism. Unable to face the decay of their own culture, imperialists looked for demons and discovered anti-white racial solidarities and pan-nationalist movements.

That sense of superiority which was the source of imperial pride and self-esteem, and which gave the Anglo-American elites internal coherence, now lacked a dynamic and a conviction. This was a major setback for the political elites of Britain and the United States, one which could be obscured for a time by the military victory in the Second World War, but not for long. The imperialist tradition that had been a major political asset had now become a source of embarrassment. The presentiment of danger discussed in this chapter was paradoxically vindicated by events. The imperialist elites saw moral authority migrate from London, Paris, Washington to a world which now claimed its right to determination its own future. Their emotional fears now had to be translated into intellectual and practical responses that could deal with Third World nationalism, in circumstances where the crisis of imperial self-image meant the old assertions of superiority were no longer an option.

3 The Social Construction of the Third World Terrorist

The overreaction to demobilised colonial soldiers discussed in the previous chapter seems positively restrained in comparison with the late twentieth-century panic about the threat allegedly posed by Third World terrorism. The Third World terrorist has emerged as the chilling Antichrist of the late twentieth-century Western imagination. The menacing spectre of Third World nationalism is further mystified by the image of half-crazed individuals ready, bomb in hand, to die for some incomprehensible cause. Media images of this phenomenon have succeeded in creating the impression that, rather than being the aggressor in the Third World, *the West is actually the victim* of these fanatical terrorists.

In the discussion of terrorism the line that divides fact from fiction is inexact. Highly ideological terms like 'international terrorism' convey the impression of some kind of globe-trotting conspiracy. Terrorism is represented as an end in itself.

The United States Government has even elevated the issue of terrorism from the individual to the national plane. Washington now designates some Third World nations as 'terrorist states'. The American list of states 'sponsoring terrorism' has included Iraq, Libya, Syria, North Korea, Cuba and Sudan. In order to earn this label it seems necessary only for a country to incur the wrath of the United States Government. For example, an American State Department survey published in April 1993 found no evidence that Sudan had conducted or sponsored specific acts of terrorism during 1992. Four months later Sudan joined the list. The criminalisation of Sudan in this way is not without historical precedent. Coincidentally, one of the first systematic campaigns of media demonisation was directed at the Mahdiyya movement in the Sudan during the nineteenth century. The humiliating defeat of General Gordon in Khartoum by the Mahdi was interpreted by the British press as a deed of 'fanatic' and 'wild hordes of dervishes'.[1] Whereas press hysteria over Mahdi fanaticism was a relatively minor subplot, international terrorism is discussed today even at the level of G-7 Conferences.

Franz Fanon has pointed to the tendency of the propaganda of the Western elite to reverse the real relations of power – the revolt against oppression is recast as a threat of fanaticism to the innocent Western power. Fanon has illustrated the criminalisation of the anti-colonial forces through his study of French propaganda directed against the Algerian liberation movement. He noted that this campaign successfully disoriented the French left, who became defensive about the 'terrorism' of the Algerians: 'The concept of barbarism appeared and it was decided that France in Algeria was fighting barbarism'.[2] His emphasis on propaganda is very much to the point. The ability to represent a particular movement as terrorist is itself the outcome of a propaganda war.

The term 'terrorist' is a loaded one – highly subjective, with aggressive connotations. A recent study of British counterinsurgency aptly remarked that one 'nation's freedom fighter is another's terrorist'.[3] In practice this symmetry is subverted by relations of power. Anybody can call anybody a terrorist. In general, however, it is those designated 'terrorist' by the great powers who suffer the consequences of living with the label.

It can be argued that public perceptions of terror are largely the outcome of propaganda campaigns aimed against anti-colonial movements. Whether or not such campaigns are successful will determine how people see the issue. This is shown by the example of Ireland in the post First World War period. In this case Britain lost the propaganda war. According to one account the IRA's propaganda was superior to that of the British. In contrast to British lethargy in this sphere, the Republican Publicity Department sent out daily news bulletins to the international media.[4] Consequently it was the British rather than the IRA who acquired a reputation for inflicting terror. Similarly, because Britain could not win the propaganda war in Palestine after the Second World War, the image of Zionist terror did not take off in the West.

As far as Britain was concerned, the Irish example was very much the exception. Within the imperial setting Britain seldom lost the propaganda war. It succeeded in establishing not only frightening images of Third World terror but also an enviable reputation for avoiding the application of excessive force. This reputation is still much in evidence in the contemporary literature. According to Anthony Low, the 'British used troops only against Communists (in Malaya) or against those who made it their business to kill (Mau Mau, EOKA, Aden's NLF)'. This is also the verdict of Mockaitis's study of British counterinsurgency. And Kathryn Tidrick is extravagant in her praise of British imperialism:

The British ambivalence towards the use and acknowledgement of armed compulsion provides one of the main themes of this book. I hope to show how the men of the empire preferred to avoid it, or if it were unavoidable ignore it – not only because they had moral reservations about physical coercion but because they believed that they were blessed with attributes of character which enabled them to prevail without it.[5]

The view that British imperial expansion and rule was essentially pacific prevails, at least in the West and from this assessment the only conclusion to be drawn was that if imperial rule was so reasonable then clearly anti-colonial violence was all the more illegitimate and senseless.

Perceptions of terror are also the product of the cumulative process of the Western criminalisation of anti-colonial resistance. A long time before the term 'terrorism' became a central category of Western political culture it was used to denigrate anti-colonial opponents. Harold Laski's 1932 lecture on 'Nationalism and the Future of Civilisation' underlines the ease with which foreign nations and peoples were discredited by the British establishment. 'Nothing seems more simple than to invent a criminal nation for the crowd', observed Laski.[6] The treatment of the revolt of Burmese peasants in 1930 by the British press epitomises Laski's point and anticipates the kind of treatment applied on a wider scale to Third World nationalism today.

The British press invariably described the Burmese peasants as primitive and irrational people. Attention was drawn to the use of magic and tattooing in a way that invites comparison with the treatment of the Mau Mau in the 1950s. According to one expert, the Burmese peasants were 'steeped in superstition'. Their 'folly about charms, magic tattoo-marks, and bullet-proof needles buried in the flesh' was offered as evidence of their primitiveness. Predictably the flipside of primitiveness was the unrestrained violence and cruelty of the Burmese peasant. The *Manchester Guardian* remarked that as 'usual with uneducated Burmans when violently excited, ferocious murders have been committed with every detail of cruelty'. *The Times* reported that the rebels were happy to 'massacre' their own compatriots, 'attacking convoys, burning villages, and committing acts of savagery'.[7]

The objective of the campaign of criminalisation was deprive the rebels of any legitimate grievances or rational motives. The *Manchester Guardian* was categorical on this point: 'the rebels' had 'shown themselves outlaws deserving no sympathy'. It concluded that they 'can plead no excuses either on political or economic grounds'. Since the rebellion had no understandable social cause, it followed that what was at stake was plain criminality. As far as the *Daily Telegraph* was concerned the Burmese were naturally disposed towards crime: 'The Burman, like many of the inhabitants of India, takes to robbery under arms when the policeman's back is turned as a duck takes to water'. They were criminals or, more specifically, terrorists. The *Manchester Guardian* informed its readers that 'it has been known to the Government for some years that there is a terrorist party in Burma which is closely associated with the terrorist movement in Bengal' and that this 'party has of late been engaged in the committing of terrorist outrages'.[8] Here in embryo was the concept of international terrorism – Burmese terrorists fraternising with their Bengali counterpart. Half a century later this form of propaganda was to achieve the status of a veritable doctrine for explaining global disorder.

It would be wrong to explain the tendency to criminalise Third World resistance as merely a dishonest form of media manipulation. The previous chapter has suggested that there was already a disposition to interpret the challenge to the West in the most extravagant terms. An examination of the available records suggests that the image of subversion and terror was prevalent not just in publicity and propaganda but also within the private worldview of officials and specialists in London and Washington. Obviously self-interest dictated misinformation, news management and downright lies. For example American intelligence had no doubt that Jomo Kenyatta was framed in the Mau Mau show trial by the British.[9] This cynicism notwithstanding, the Americans and the British truly believed the underlying themes in their public presentation of anti-colonial struggles. Through a consideration of the main themes and experiences that helped shape their beliefs, this chapter will seek to isolate the epistemological foundation of the image of the Third World terrorist.

Elite Perspectives

It is possible to see the presentiment of disorder examined in Chapter 2 as an emotional reaction shaped by the prevailing intellectual currents. The presentiment of disorder was shaped by intellectual influences that dominated the outlook of Anglo-American officials and experts concerned with colonial societies. The sense of foreboding about anti-colonial and nationalist movements had little to do with the experience of interacting with the peoples of Africa or Asia. Instead, the intellectual framework used by Western experts to interpret colonial societies was founded on the experience of their own cultures. The intellectual tradition associated with the imperialist outlook tended to foster an intense suspicion towards the masses in the colonies. During the late nineteenth and early twentieth centuries both conservative and liberal studies of nationalism, political parties and other social movements stressed their unstable, irrational and destructive character.

At the level of imperial sensibility, perceptions and attitudes were in part a response to the cumulative experience of Empire. But they were also shaped by an intellectual legacy that moulded the imperial mind. In a sense the prevailing attitudes towards anti-colonial mass movements had little to do with the colonies. The intellectual tradition in Britain would have encouraged the imperial mind's intense suspicion of anti-colonial nationalism anyway, regardless of what went on in the colonial world. The prevailing studies of nationalism and of social movements characteristically portrayed them in terms which stressed their instability, irrationalism and destructiveness.

Within the Anglo-American social sciences from the late nineteenth century the negative reaction to mass movements is palpable. Writers on both sides of the Atlantic emphasised the volatility of the urban mob, its vulnerability to manipulation by the media and its ultimate destructiveness. Political conservatives in particular regarded the masses as an essentially primitive and unintelligent force incapable of exercising reason.

The crowd psychologist Gustave Le Bon personified the anti-mass outlook of the Anglo-American elite. According to Le Bon, the conditions of mass society wore away the recently adopted forms of civilised behaviour to expose the 'savage' and 'primitive' survivals beneath. According to Nye, for Le Bon and his co-thinkers 'the crowd mind was presumed to reflect "atavistic" traits or "primordial sentiments" deeply embedded in the primitive heritage of the race'.[10] Le Bon argued that these sentiments which existed in a pure form in primitive societies, could reassert themselves within the Western urban crowd. Accordingly reason would always be vanquished by passion:

> It is not even necessary to descend so low as primitive beings to obtain an insight into the utter powerlessness of reasoning when it has to fight against sentiment. Let us merely call to mind how tenacious, for centuries long, have been religious superstitions in contradiction with the simplest logic.[11]

In other words, savage and irrational impulses were rooted in the human condition. And collection of individuals into crowds would undermine the restraining influence of civilisation and bring to the surface primordial sentiments.

Although no longer respectable, crowd psychology is not without influence today, especially in the popular media. The uninformed crowd cleverly manipulated by a demagogue is a motif that reoccurs in a variety of discussions – from considerations of the power of the media to considerations of Third World movements. The *Daily Mail's* representation of the relationship between Saddam Hussain and the Iraqi masses is apposite in this respect:

> Saddam is now activating his most potent weapon – the fanaticism which lies like a time-bomb beneath the surface of Islamic society. It can always be detonated by a rabble-rousing leader.[12]

The rabble-rousing leader or the demagogue is the other side of the coin to the crowd. Early political sociology was sceptical of the ability of the masses to elect leaders who represented their interest. The early works of Ostrogorski and Lowell gave prominence to the boss. Michels's classic account of social democratic parties stressed the importance of oligarchical tendencies.[13] Some sociologists continued to promote crowd theories in the post Second World War period. The British sociologist Maurice Ginsberg maintained in the 1960s that 'in crowds the individual is, as Le Bon points out, apt to lose his sense of responsibility'.[14]

Le Bon's reaction to mass society was in many ways extreme and idiosyncratic. But his underlying fear of the masses was widely shared. An explosion of studies of 'public opinion' during the first three decades of this century indicate a growing alarm about this phenomenon.[15] It is difficult to find any studies that have anything positive to say about public opinion, crowds or masses. There is a clear elitist consensus which unites virtually the entire political spectrum. For conservative writers, the entry of the masses into social and political life could only pose a threat to civilised society, whereas those from a liberal/left perspective saw the masses as a danger to democracy.

Often it was the liberal disappointment with the 'failure' of democracy that fostered the reaction against the masses. The American commentator, Walter Lippman provided the classic statement in his 1922 study, *Public Opinion*: he warned that the proportion of the electorate which was 'absolutely illiterate' was much larger than suspected and that these people who were 'mentally children or barbarians' were natural targets of manipulators. This view of public opinion dominated Anglo-American social science in the interwar period. Often it conveyed the patronising assumption that public opinion does not know what is in its best interests. As one American sociologist argued in 1929: 'public opinion is often very cruel to those who struggle most unselfishly for the public welfare'.[16]

British liberal commentators also assumed an unfavourable view of mass politics. Hobson the well-known liberal anti-imperialist expressed a clear disdain for the urban masses in his denunciation of jingoism. His description of the 'atmosphere' of jingoism provided a clear picture of what he feared:

> A coarse patriotism fed by the wildest rumours and the most violent appeals to hate and the animal lust of blood, passes by quick contagion through the crowded life of cities, and recommends itself everywhere by the satisfaction it affords to sensational cravings.[17]

The influential British political theorist Graham Wallas shared Hobson's disappointment of mass democracy. His description of working-class women being mobilised to vote by canvasser during a London County Council election conveys a barely concealed contempt:

> About half of them were women, with broken straw hats, pallid faces, and untidy hair. All were dazed and bewildered, having been snatched away in carriages or motors from the making of match-boxes, button holes, or cheap furniture, or from the public house, or, since it was Saturday evening, from bed.[18]

Here were people who were barely fit to vote. The conclusion derived from this argument was that mass democracy based on people who were easily manipulated by demagogues was a direct threat to democracy.

One important trend in Anglo-American political science was the discussion of what to do with a public that could not be relied on to grasp its own best interests. Just as missionaries claimed to act as trustees on behalf of ignorant savages, so elite theorists assumed the role of guardians of the masses. The most favoured solution was to preserve the existing structures of tradition. Slowing down change, preserving tradition, or at least religion and the family, were seen as antidotes to mass psychology. As late as 1963 the prominent liberal American political scientist was celebrating the democratic consequences of retaining traditional institutions like the monarchy: 'thus we have the absurd fact that ten out of the twelve stable European and English speaking democracies are monarchies'.[19]

A key component of the elitist perception of the masses was the traditionalist argument that change leading to 'maladjustment' would provoke destructive mass reaction. That is why someone like Le Bon, with no colonial experience, could argue against assimilation both within France and the colonies. He feared that if the restraining influence of the traditional order was removed, then the 'barbarian hordes' of the colonies and the 'crowds' of Europe would revolt against civilisation. He warned of the danger of reforming colonial life:

> We must not forget at last that the exact hour that definite decadence began in the great Roman Empire was when Rome gave the rights of citizens to the barbarians.[20]

The breakdown of tradition, the transformation of 'barbarian' people into modern Western roles would weaken all social restraints. It was this fear that guided the thinking of Western observers towards the emerging colonial masses. A kind of Durkheimian fear of moral collapse saturates the pages of British and American sociological literature on the subject.

In their deliberation on the masses in Europe, elite theorists often drew self-conscious analogies with the situation in the colonies. So when William Booth, the founder of the Salvation Army wrote of the poor as the 'Darkest England' his readers would not have missed the analogy with 'Darkest Africa'. Walter Bagehot explicitly linked the morality of the English poor with 'savages':

> if men differ in anything they differ in the ... delicacy of their moral intuitions ... we need not go as far as savages to learn that lesson; we need only talk to the English poor or to our servants, and we shall be taught it very completely. The lower classes in civilised countries, like all classes in uncivilised countries are clearly wanting in the nicer part of those feelings which, taken together, we call the *sense* of morality.[21]

Those influenced by this tradition – and Bagehot was widely read in the universities well into the 1930s – had fairly negative attitudes about the morality of the 'uncivilised'. Such attitudes were an integral part of the self-knowledge of the American and British elite. Those educated in this outlook were sure that they knew what the problem was when they arrived at Whitehall or the State department, even before they picked up their first intelligence report on an anti-colonial movement.

Nationalism as Passion

As a mass movement nationalism was feared as a reaction not susceptible to rational restraint. It is important to recall that by the early part of this century the liberal Anglo-American intellectual universe regarded the concept of nationalism in terms that were ambivalent and often negative. These attitudes were not a response to developments in the colonies; they were part of a reaction to the experience of Europe. Nationalism was identified as the main cause of conflict and war from the Balkans to central and Western Europe.

This reaction was connected to the perception that nationalist movements which were previously comfortably controlled by the elites had now acquired a mass character. It was not the concept of the nation itself that Western intellectuals now called into question – that remained the foundation of their society. Nor were they at all antagonistic towards nationalism of the traditional, elitist variety. It was the nationalism of the masses which now attracted fear and loathing. Intellectuals denounced it as destructive, irrational and ultimately anti-democratic. By the 1930s it is difficult to find a wholehearted intellectual defence of nationalism.

Of course there was another double standard at work. The Anglo-American literature tended to make something of an exception for its own nationalisms. Invariably the unhealthy nationalism of others was counterposed to the uniqueness of the British experience. Marjery Perham wrote of the special qualities of British nationalism due to 'our exceptional unity, our island position, and the confidence arising from our power' which 'may have bred in us an unconscious kind of nationalism, one that seldom needed to assert or even to know itself'.[22] This self-flattering portrait of British nationalism was held up as the fine exception to the rest. Wallas was more generous than most. He praised the nationalism of Bismarck and Mazzini but warned that it was 'becoming less and less possible to accept it as a solution for the problems of the twentieth century'.[23]

The studies that would have influenced American and British officials from the 1930s onwards all tended to treat nationalism as a threat to stability. One of the most influential and often-cited studies of nationalism in Anglo-American scholarship in the interwar period concluded that it was 'either ignorant and prejudiced or inhuman or jaundiced … Nationalism is artificial and it is far from ennobling; in a word it is *patriotic snobbery*'.[24] This assessment expressed the reaction of the liberal intelligentsia to the devastating consequence of the First World War. Hobson, writing in the 1930s summed it all up when he warned of the 'chief perils and disturbances associated with the aggressive nationalism of today'.[25] Laski warned that the 'excesses' of nationalism 'will destroy civilization' unless curbed.[26]

This negative reaction to the phenomenon of nationalism was not restricted to a handful of pacifist thinkers. A study of nationalism published under the auspices of the policy-oriented Royal Institute of International Affairs (RIIA) in 1939 began from the premise that 'contemporary developments of nationalism appear to threaten the very future of civilization'. The study conceded that nationalism had a 'good reputation' in the nineteenth century but warned that this 'should not blind us to its constant aggression and incitement to war'. The RIIA's study of the 'Colonial Problem' put the emphasis on the possible danger that the development of national 'self-consciousness may transfer to colonial areas the militant nationalism from which we suffer in Europe'.[27] It is useful to recall that the RIIA, more commonly known as Chatham House, acted as something of a think-tank for Whitehall.

This negative conceptualisation of mass nationalism was given a powerful boost by the experience of Second World War, and by the linkage which was consequently widely made between fascism and 'frustrated nationalism'. Virtually all the major studies of nationalism of the 1940s are in some sense a reaction to the Nazi episode. Many expressed a fear of mass nationalism as a powerful totalitarian and destructive force. Studies stressed the potential of nationalism for causing destruction and even genocide. For Namier it was an 'obsession' which brought ruin to Europe, an 'expression of social and political maladjustment'. As a movement it was 'akin in nature to the horde'. According to this totalitarian interpretation of nationalism, a tradition that retains its influence to this day, it 'played a major role in fortifying both Nazism and Stalinism'.[28]

In the 1940s, the themes of irrationalism, destructiveness and totalitarianism were supplemented by a new concern – the intrinsically *anti-Western* or *non-Western* character of nationalism. One typical study of the period argued that 'Western civilization in most of its aspects, and especially in the sphere of politics, is fundamentally opposed to the claims and practices of nationalism'.[29] As the problem of nationalism was relocated from the West to the East so it became fashionable to counterpose the two.

The already existing intellectual assessment of European nationalism adapted to the growth of the Third World variety by developing the couplet of mature Western versus immature Eastern nationalism. In this reaction to Third World nationalism there was an unconscious tendency to minimise the irrational aspects of the European variety and to exaggerate it in relation to the eastern forms. Hans Kohn's classic text of the 1940s praised Western nationalism as a mature one which adhered

to a basically 'rational and universal concept of political liberty' and looked
'towards the city of the future'. In contrast, Eastern nationalism was
'basically founded on history, on monuments, on graveyards, even
harking back to the mysteries of ancient times and of tribal solidarity'.[30]

The East–West dichotomy of two sorts of nationalism became an
accepted part of Western political theory. In the 1940s, the East–West
model allowed observers legitimately to view the emerging anti-colonial
nationalism as particularly venal. Reports from the colonies continually stressed this point. An analysis of the situation in East Africa
observed:

> There is no widespread ... demand for self-government or any con-
> sciousness of national unity such as was characteristic of European
> nationalist movements. Such nationalist agitation as does exist in
> East Africa is inspired and shaped by individual agitators and associ-
> ations aiming ... at securing political prominence for themselves.[31]

When colonial nationalist were not depicted as self-serving scoundrels
they were dismissed as mentally unbalanced. According to a Foreign
Office assessment of Asian nationalism, 'the fear of political or economic
"colonialism" is all-pervading and often strictly psychopathic'.[32]

The East–West couplet informs most of the key studies on nationalism in the post Second World War period. Gunnar Myrdal's classic
Asian Drama counterposes the rational nationalism of Europe to the
irrational one of Asia. Myrdal wrote that in 'South Asia inhibitions and
obstacles to rational thinking are much greater than they had been in
Europe' and concluded that this 'cannot be without influence on South
Asian nationalism'. According to Myrdal the two nationalisms possess
different qualities: 'Thus, in spite of all the parallels to European nationalism, the new nationalism in South Asia is something very different'.[33]
What Myrdal is striving to say is that the object of the discussion in
South Asia is not really nationalism in the western sense.

From the 1960s onwards, consideration by Western academics of the
nationalism of the East came increasingly to be conducted through terms
that inflated its differences with the European experience. The focus
was on the inconsistency between the quality of Eastern nationalism
and democratic aspirations. Plamenatz distinguishes between the nationalism of those who are 'culturally equipped in ways that favour success
and excellence', that is Western nationalism, and the nationalism that
is 'imitative and hostile to the models it imitates, and is apt to be
illiberal'. A recent study by Smith distinguished between the non-
Western model of an 'ethnic' conception of a nation, whose

'distinguishing feature is its emphasis on a community of birth and native culture' and the rational Western one where the individual could 'choose' to which nation 'he or she belonged'.[34]

In recent years the counterposition between Eastern and Western nationalisms has been further exaggerated and is the intellectual foundation for the view that Eastern nationalisms of various sorts represent the main danger to world peace. This certainly is the underlying supposition behind Fukuyama's 'End of History' thesis. While warning of the danger of unstable nationalisms, he seems extravagantly complacent about the Western variety.[35] The implication of Fukuyama's argument is to transform Third World nationalism into the negative antithesis of the Western one.

Nationalists as Nazis

Many influential Western authors expressed the hope that after the defeat of Hitler nationalism would be discredited and become a spent force in Europe. E.H. Carr advanced the opinion that the Second World War signified the 'climax' of nationalism. Others chose to ignore the reality of nationalism in the West and concentrated their fire against such movements in the colonies. The former Governor of Nigeria, Lord Milverton wrote somewhat contemptuously that:

> it is a curious paradox that Africa and Asia are being swept by nationalistic aspirations at a time when the national idea is becoming out-moded in the West and the civilized world is groping its way towards wider conceptions – a supranational recognition of the unity of mankind.[36]

It could be argued that the post Second World War fashion for denouncing nationalism as 'out-moded' was at least indirectly linked to the manifest challenge which its growth in the Third World represented to imperial interests. This was no doubt one of the motives inspiring the new critiques of nationalism. However, operating at a more fundamental level was the response to the discrediting of nationalism in its European context. It was the Nazi experience which dealt the fatal blow to the intellectual case for nationalism.

In many contributions mass nationalism was presented as the cause of Nazism. Elitist theories saw the Nazi experience as confirmation of the destructive power of crowds. Hitler appeared as the vindication of Le Bon. One British writer explained:

Paradoxically enough, it is to fascism that we have to turn in order to find the political movement and expression most exclusively representative of the real masses – to find in other words, the mass movement *par excellence*, the supreme example of political collectivism.

Karl Popper, the right-wing scourge of collectivism agreed – nationalism appealed to 'tribal instincts, passions and prejudice and dislike of individual responsibility'. And Fritz Stern of Columbia University reminded his readers that the 'success of national socialism in Germany should not obscure the fact that the nationalist attack on modern culture is a general Western phenomenon that preceded and has outlived national socialism'.[37]

The new negative intellectual view of nationalism and its association with Nazism reflected an elitist fear of the masses. The tenuous link between Nazism and nationalism was that both had a mass and collective character. It was as if mass action was itself inherently illiberal and anti-democratic. The advantage of the nationalist/Nazi synthesis was that it allowed the imperialist mind to mobilise the legitimacy gained through the war against fascism in a campaign to deprive anti-colonial movements of their credibility. All of this encouraged the imperial imagination to rediscover fanatics from the Balkans and Nazis from Germany in the colonies.

The contemporary equation of Saddam Hussain with Hitler has a long and respectable history. Since the outbreak of the Second World War any militant nationalist movement that could not plausibly be labelled communist could expect to be characterised as fascist. It is almost as if the Hitler/Nazi image seemed too good to pass up. Some movements, such as those of the nationalists in Burma or Argentina, could even be labelled as communist and fascist at the same time. One study rediscovered European political trends in Burmese nationalism and suggested that there was a 'marked change in political thought' as 'nineteenth century liberalism tended to give way to twentieth century communist and fascist ideologies'. Another study argued that Peronism in Argentina 'cannot accurately be called Communist, Nazi or Fascist', because it has characteristics of all three. A study of the APRA movement in Peru conducted by the British Foreign Office could not make up its mind whether APRA was 'communist influenced' or contained the 'germs of fascism'.[38] The assertion of Egyptian autonomy by Nasser led to predictable comparisons with Hitler.

The intellectual framework for interpreting nationalism as it prevailed in the late 1940s disposed colonial administrators to find Nazi terror in the most unlikely places. Walter Crocker came across it during his sojourn in India in the period leading up to independence:

> In Mahatma Gandhi's land of *Ahmisa* and *Satyagraha* I found myself back in prewar Nazi Germany. There were the same massed processions, the same screaming press from which objectivity and decency alike been abolished, the same murder-inciting speeches, the mobs, the flags, the quasi-military parades, the special salutes, the uniforms, the oaths and the *Heils* (Jai Hind).[39]

From Nuremberg-style parades in India it was a short journey to discovering stormtroopers in the exotic location of the Solomon Islands. Here the Resident Commissioner, O.C. Noel, reported that the 'mystic appeal' of Maasina Rule provided a 'parallel with the strange fervour that swiftly swept over Germany and resulted in the promotion of the Third Reich'. Noel backed up his account by citing the views of a Mr Cameron, 'who has a fair knowledge of Germany and the German language'. Cameron's description of areas dominated by Maasina Rule showed this 'knowledge'. He observed: 'Barring natural differences of climate, economic and geographical this [Maalu] district bears an astounding resemblance to a National Socialistic Gau during the heyday of that party's power in the Third Reich.'[40]

The strength of the linkage between Nazi imagery and anti-colonial protest is confirmed by the fact that even liberal and left-wing critics of imperialism were influenced by it. So Peter Evans, a left-wing Irish lawyer expelled from Kenya for attempting to intervene in the Kenyatta trial, allegedly confided in private that 'Jomo Kenyatta if left to himself would produce a kind of African Nazism'.[41] If this was the sentiment held by a left-wing lawyer it is not surprising that in the 1940s and 1950s the despatches of colonial officials and the articles of contemporary observers are full of references to Nazi-type metaphors. A study of African reaction to the West in *International Affairs* warns that to 'gain power over the tribesmen', nationalists 'must bring out the darker side on men's natures'. The author adds: 'Hitler has shown how successfully the darker side of even Western man's nature can be brought out; how much more easily could this apply to tribal man.'[42] The expectation that African nationalism must involve the manipulation of destructive urges on a Hitlerian scale had the character of a commonsense observation in the discussion of the 1940s and the early 1950s.

It is important to emphasise that the intellectual foundations of this response had their roots in the European experience. The elaboration of the East–West couplet merely expanded on already existing ideas.

So, by the 1940s, the negative assessment of nationalism and the
tendency to draw parallels between the destructive legacy of fascism and
anti-colonial politics came quite naturally to those educated in the
Anglo-American tradition of elite theory. This intellectual disposition
was at the time almost all-pervasive. Consequently, even more critical
and questioning observers and scholars would find it difficult to empathise
with the national aspirations of colonial peoples.[43] From this standpoint
such unreasonable movements needed to be repressed – the politics of
force made sense.

As Maladjustment

If nationalism expressed irrational tendencies in Europe than the same
force in the colonies was seen to be positively menacing. Western
social theory was at first bemused by the fervour with which colonial
people sought to defend their customs and uphold their identities and
sense of the past. This emerging nationalist response, which was routine
among Irish intellectuals learning Gaelic in the late nineteenth century
or East Europeans inventing traditional customs, struck many Western
observers as curious when it occurred in the colonies. There were some
sensitive exceptions to this ethnocentric trend.[44] The dominant tone,
however, was a defensive one. The defence of custom and identity in
the colonies was invariably understood as a direct rejection of the West.
Therefore it was interpreted as a problem.

   Malinowski, probably the most influential of the British-based anthropologists, who regularly lectured officials in the colonial service argued
that the 'new African type of nationalism, of racial feeling, and of
collective opposition to Western culture' was 'of the greatest importance
for all studies in contact and change'.[45] Observers less sensitive to
colonial societies tended to see in this rejection of Western customs proof
of cultures that were fundamentally its opposite. The East–West couplet
of nationalism was recycled as a rigid counterposition between traditional and modern societies. The literature of the 1930s, 1940s and 1950s
demonstrates a consistent tendency to exaggerate the difference between
Western and colonial peoples and their outlook. In social theory this
tendency was articulated through the mechanical counterposition of a
series of couplets. Evans-Pritchard wrote tongue-in-cheek: 'we are
rational, primitive peoples prelogical, living in a world of dreams and
make believe, of mystery and awe; we are capitalist, they are communist;
we are monogamous, they are promiscuous; we are monotheists, they
are fetishists, animists, pre-animists, or what have you, and so on'.[46]

Even more rigorous and enlightened academics were drawn to a 'two different worlds' approach. The anthropologist Meyer Fortes, writing in the *Fabian Colonial Essays* underlined the 'great gulf between the qualitative make-up of most primitive societies' and 'Euro-American civilization' as he enumerated the usual couplets that counterpose the primitive to the modern.[47] Even relatively sensitive accounts of non-Western cultures tended to consider their subject matter through concepts that were unlikely to be applied to investigation of European social phenomena. Nationalism in the colonial context was likely to be described as racial feeling, racial consciousness, Ethiopianism, Africanism or nativistic. Take Ralph Linton's very influential concept of 'nativistic movements'. Unlike some of his colleagues, Linton was able to elaborate some of the common characteristics of European and non-European social movements. Yet his concept of nativistic movement, which he defined as 'any conscious organised attempt on the part of a society's members to revive or perpetuate selected aspects of its culture' reveals more about his own preoccupations than the movements under study.[48]

Linton's definition of a nativistic movement could cover virtually every European nationalist movement to date. Yet it is rare to find studies which isolate the attempt to revive past culture as *the* distinctive theme of European nationalism. It seems as if, in their investigations of colonial movements, Linton and other social scientists could not quite bring themselves to concede that what they were studying was a political nationalist response to Western domination. Instead the discussion was obscured through consideration of 'culture clashes' and 'acculturation'. Europeans had *nationalism* and 'they' had *nativistic* movements. Although seldom brought into an explicit conceptual relation to each other, they existed as an unstated analytic couplet.

Whatever the particular couplet under consideration, the focus of intellectual endeavour was to underline the irrational, mystical/hysterical and therefore potentially uncontrollable aspects of colonial social movements. Third World social movements are seldom political; they are 'cargo cults' or religious protests. Edward Said's account of *Orientalism,* whereby Arab national feeling always 'assumes a religious aspect' in the Western literature, is of relevance to studies of the colonial situation.[49]

Investigations of political, social and religious movements all centred on their irrational content. The assertion of 'tradition' and 'identity' in the colonial world was explained as flowing from a 'need' that was at once psychological and non-rational. An article in *Corona*, the British colonial service's house-magazine suggests that the development of 'nativistic movements' like Maasina Rule was 'conditioned by factors of stress, frustration, and misunderstanding of European institutions'.[50] These confused psychological reactions – colonial people have an incorrigible habit of failing to understand European institutions – were decoded by Western observers to suggest that the problem was their state of mind. The problem was variously described as the difficulty of adapting to modern circumstances or to frustration with some aspect of social change. Malinowski's thesis that 'change as a rule means at least maladjustment' provided a framework where anti-colonial protest could be depicted as expressions of frustration.[51] Terms like 'frustrated nationalism' or 'crisis cult' appropriately summed up the approach. From this perspective anti-colonial movements were a reaction to their own failure to cope with the exigencies of change. This was the thesis of the imperial publicist Elspeth Huxley in her survey in the *Corona* of the 'many fanatical, half-crazy, quasi-religious cults'. Her verdict was that these reactions 'personify a subconscious revolt against the growing complexity of life, the too-quick pace of change, the indigestibility of great chunks of Westernism'.[52]

The maladjustment thesis allowed for an excessively psychological interpretation, where any manifestation of social unrest could be dismissed as the product of unstable minds. One early account of Maasina Rule wrote of 'huge meetings' which were 'accompanied by mass hysteria'.[53] No evidence of any examples of hysteria were offered, for the simple reason that this affliction did not exist. However, from this intellectual perspective, the accusation did not have to be proved since the action of maladjusted individuals was bound to be irrational. Reports of anti-colonial movements often warned of the danger posed by an explosion of a collective psychosis. A discussion of the security of East and Central Africa in June 1948 was worried about 'dangerous religious outbursts'. It warned of the 'added danger of an increase in fanatical religious sects' which could be 'used for political purposes'.[54] Here were unspecified dangers stemming from the difficulty of controlling unstable minds. A Foreign Office study, *The Problem of Nationalism*, reduced the issue to psychology in the following way:

> Exploited or dissatisfied nationalism produces a state of mind in which any sense of grievance, injustice or inferiority is magnified out of all proportion. This can lead to a state of unbalance amounting in the worst cases to hysteria. This state of mind is highly infectious.[55]

Reduced to a state of mind that was also infectious, nationalism was reconstituted as a medical problem.

Explanations of Asian nationalism were often cast in an entirely psychological mould. Typically political and cultural responses were described as psychological ones. The Foreign Office's Information Policy Department's discussion of the 'principal psychological factors which influence the situation' offered the following as an example: 'Anti-imperialism and Asian nationalism which leads many extreme nationalists in South East Asia to deny any coincidence of interest with the West'. The perception that there may be a conflict of interest between Britain and its Asian colonies is here diagnosed as a psychological factor. It appears that to dwell on imperialist domination is a necessary symptom of a psychological disorder. The discussion routinely uses medical terms to describe political responses.[56]

The diagnosis of anti-colonial protest as a medical condition acquired an extreme form in relation to the Mau Mau. Even a liberal text on racism could write with conviction that 'there can be little doubt that Mau Mau is the symptom of a sick society'. The author accepts far-fetched analogies between Mau Mau violence and the atrocities of Belsen and seems to suggest that the problem is that of human decay.[57] As mass psychological disturbances reacting to frustrations, anti-colonial movements could not claim to be legitimate attempts to solve social problems. These reactions could be dismissed as confusions or as an escape from reality.

The Marginal Man

Anthropologists and other academic experts in touch with the Colonial Office tended to portray manifestations of 'nativism' as a reversion to, or revitalisation of, past traditions. The impulse for reviving the past was explained as a reaction to what was often called a 'spiritual', 'moral' or 'cultural' vacuum. According to this thesis, Westernisation had created a maladjusted society. It had undermined or destroyed the old traditions without replacing them with a viable modern alternative. This thesis was widely advocated by both popular and scholarly studies of the colonial situation.

The writings of the historian A.J. Toynbee provide an eloquent exposition of the spiritual vacuum thesis. Toynbee's own version of this argument was to call for the preservation of old traditions because he feared that Western civilisation in 'tropical territories' produced a 'social and spiritual void'. As a result, the indigenous people were 'left spiritually naked and abashed'. Toynbee feared that the wrong kind of influences would fill this spiritual void.[58] In the past, these arguments led to the conservative conclusions of the imperial policy of indirect rule. Malinowski himself called for 'indirect development' in order to avoid the consequences of maladjustment.[59] By the late 1940s the spiritual void thesis was transformed into a *moral condemnation* of anti-colonial protest.

In the social sciences the spiritual vacuum thesis was closely linked with the theory of the *marginal man*. This theory, explored first by the American sociologist Robert Park and fully elaborated by his student Everett Stonequist, was one of the most influential approaches to the study of reactions to change in colonial societies. Heavily influenced by the British imperial perspective of seeking to conserve tradition in order to minimise the effects of change, Stonequist developed a theory which explained the different reactions to Western domination as the product of maladjustment.

The marginal man is the product of two worlds but belongs to neither. According to Stonequist the most 'obvious type of marginal man is the person of mixed racial ancestry'. Other examples are the 'Westernised' or 'Missionary' or 'Detribalised' native. Such people are no longer able to carry on with traditional life, nor are they fully accepted into Western culture. Thus marginal men are also maladjusted. It is this psychological dilemma which explains why this group is drawn toward anti-colonial agitation. Nationalist politics becomes the means through which the maladjusted marginal men cope with life. Consequently anti-colonial agitation is not so much a response to imperialist domination but the attempt of maladjusted individuals to adjust to their circumstances. Stonequist wrote:

> His uncertain social position intensifies his concern about status. His anxiety to solve his personal problem forces him to take an interest in the racial problem as a whole.[60]

The driving force of anti-colonial politics is the psychological frustration of the marginal men. Stonequist's stress on adjustment leaves colonial reality as unproblematic. In this apologetic theory it is the frustrated individual that constitutes the problem. It is not idealism, political conviction or nationalist motivation that drives anti-colonial movements but the petty ego of the maladjusted personality.

Said's description of Western representation of the Orient focused on the recurrent theme whereby the:

oriental is imagined to feel his world threatened by a superior civilisation; yet his motives are impelled, not by some positive desire for freedom, political independence, or cultural achievement *in their own terms* but instead by rancour or jealous malice.[61]

The spiritual void of the African and the Asian suggested personalities that had undergone a cosmic moral collapse. This was not a possible inference but a central element of the concept of the marginal man. Robert Ezra Park, probably the most prominent American sociologist of the interwar years and a former President of the American Sociological Society, explicitly raised questions about the moral integrity of the marginal man. He noted how the Christian convert in Asia and Africa exhibited 'spiritual instability, intensified self-consciousness, restlessness, and malaise'. The mind of the marginal man was in 'moral turmoil'.[62]

Crowd psychology and discussions of the European urban mob were recycled to promote the image of the moral wasteland of anti-colonial protest. The theories which dwelt on the irrationalism of anti-colonial action, nativism, crisis cults and spiritual voids lent intellectual coherence to Western prejudices which regarded those experiencing these processes as decadent or morally deviant. The link that Durkheim established between maladjustment and moral malaise and instability was applied to colonial societies in the form of a condemnation.[63] So Asians emerging from 'medieval civilisation' in the Far East had become 'disoriented' and had developed an irrational hostility to colonialism. Such disturbed minds lacked the accepted standards of morality. A report from the British Embassy in Teheran wrote with conviction:

> it is essential to begin by recognising that 99% of the Persian populace are mentally thorough-going asiatics – that is to say, what they understand most clearly is force and success. They have practically no social consciousness.[64]

Altruism, sense of social responsibility, duty or compassion are just some of the qualities that simply do not exist in the spiritual vacuum in colonial societies.

Academics as well as imperial officials tended to interpret the consequence of maladjustment as that of moral depravity. The breakdown of civic virtues is the theme of the anthropologist, Meyer Fortes's 1944 essay on the colonial situation:

> The religious and legal sanctions of right conduct have become ambiguous, and the common symptoms of a maladjusted social system – crime, prostitution, corruption, and unbridled acquisitive-

ness – have become prominent to an extent never known in the traditional social order ... There is no such thing as a civic conscience or civic pride.[65]

If a relatively detached anthropologist interpreted the attitude of colonial people in moral terms, officials and administrators were likely to condemn what they saw with a far more extravagant vocabulary.

The model that emerged was one which projected the scenario of change leading to the breakdown of tradition, which in turn results in the erosion of social control. Moral collapse is the inevitable consequence of this process. According to a standard account from the 1950s:

> Disruption has taken place in traditional codes of laws and morals, resulting in a disturbing increase in the signs and symptoms of an unstable society. These include high rates of delinquency and crime, disharmony and breakdown of family relationships, alcoholism, mental ill-health, as well as aggressive and violent behaviour of which *Mau Mau* is probably the most terrible example.[66]

By this time Mau Mau symbolised the moral depravity of those who inhabited the spiritual vacuum of anti-colonialism.

The 'semi-educated' or 'detribalised' colonial is the natural offspring of the prevailing spiritual void. The demagogues of European crowd psychology now reappear as articulate critics of colonialism. They are represented in the imperial mind as desperate individuals capable of any action because they are so totally uprooted. Malinowski, more sympathetic then most to the 'African in transition' warned that 'we are faced with the birth and growth of new forces of nationalism and racialism which may be hostile, unmanageable, and dangerous in the long run'.[67] In Asia, the extremism of the intellectual is the product of a sense of inferiority towards the West. 'The absence of spiritual continuity and harmony creates a loss of faith and a cultural vacuum', according to a study of 'The Mind of Asia'.[68]

The representation of colonial politicians as unwholesome and evil is intermixed with hints that the gullible masses need to be protected from them. Thus British survey of Indian nationalism 1919 pointedly remarked that the Brahmin 'who still constitutes 90 per cent of the *intelligentsia*, cares not a row of pins for the "voiceless millions" over whom he has been wont to lord it in the past'. 'Nevertheless', concluded the author, 'your Brahmin "democrat" – a contradiction in terms, by the way – is shrewd enough to see that the voiceless millions, organised as mobs, may serve his purpose admirably'.[69] Kathrene Mayo, whose hugely successful books on India widely influenced the American public's perceptions of the subcontinent during the interwar years, conveyed the same message. She bemoaned the fact that there were 'few signs' among 'Indian public men, of concern for the status of the masses'. According to Mayo, it was Britain who was 'doing practically all of whatever is done for the comfort of sad old Mother India'.[70] The need to protect the Third World from its political leaders is a theme that endures in one form or another to this day.

A Moral Condemnation

At least outwardly, at the level of political rhetoric, during the 1940s the international climate had begun to respond favourably to anti-colonial claims. The Western media in particular adopted a hostile stance towards imperialism and demanded a positive response to the aspiration for self-determination and equality. In this climate the elitist intellectual tradition and political culture discussed previously could not openly be expressed.

However, in the new egalitarian climate the assumptions of racial superiority did not disappear, they merely became less explicit. For example the theories of maladjustment, marginal man and spiritual vacuums allowed the relationship of superiority and inferiority to be recast in moral terms. In this way the motives of anti-colonial activists were called into question. Academic experts on both sides of the Atlantic helped establish the image of the self-serving or irrational anti-imperialist agitator. In Britain they were on hand to confirm this perspective and to feed the Colonial Office with arguments that exaggerated the sordid aspects of anti-colonial movements. Thus the British anthropologist Audrey Richards, writing from the vantage point of the East African Institute of Social Research in Uganda, reinforced Whitehall prejudice when she reported that the disturbances of 1949 were caused by 'disappointed undertrained frustrated "business men" rather than by nationalists in the original sense of the word'.[71] It seemed that nationalists in the 'original' sense simply did not exist in the colonies. Instead they were 'unrepresentative' individuals who 'claimed' to be nationalists but who were in fact driven by base and unworthy motives. The movements they led were 'unhealthy' and often positively evil.

The view of the morally inferior colonial was firmly established in the imperialist imagination. Its political culture and intellectual tradition inexorably led towards that conclusion. Thus we find an expert in the British Colonial Office proposing that reports be obtained from psychologists and sociologists 'with a view to determining whether any thing can be done to raise the moral standards of the new African society'.[72] This smug assumption of moral superiority helped forge the conviction that in the colonies the West faced *unworthy* opponents. It is this systematic moral condemnation of anti-colonial movements that helps establish an audience in the West for the myth of the Third World terrorist. Lacking 'our' moral integrity, '*they*' are capable of the worst.

4 From Containment to Accommodation: the Anglo-American Management of African Nationalism

So far our discussion has focused on one side of the story. It has concentrated on the emotional reactions and intellectual dispositions that moulded the Western response to the emergence of anti-colonial politics. By the 1940s the tendency to criminalise and morally to condemn these movements had become a central component of Western political culture. However, it was not enough to condemn Third World nationalism. By the 1940s anti-imperialist movements posed a major challenge to the West's authority and political legitimacy. Practical measures to deal with the challenge were now required.

By the end of the Second World War the international climate of opinion had shifted against the culture of imperialism. Imperialists were on the defensive and colonialism was discredited. Under these circumstances the West found it difficult to contest the demand for national independence at the ideological level. Whereas American and British politicians felt that they were able to counter the ideology of the Soviet bloc, they were far less able to combat the demands of anti-imperialism.

The tasks facing imperialist politicians and intellectuals after the Second World War were formidable. Most of the principles associated with imperialist politics stood discredited. As one account recalled, after the experience of the Second World War 'racism joined imperialism and jingoism as obsolescent ideologies'.[1] Most of the working assumptions of the imperial mentality could no longer be advanced openly. Many government officials were taken aback by the strength of anti-colonial opinion. At a meeting of the Far East Publicity Committee in 1950, a representative of the British Foreign Office reported that:

> Intense nationalist propaganda during the last year has led to a strong bias against Colonialism of all sorts. Any suggestion of racial discrimination even against black Africans for whom a certain scorn was

felt, led to indignation. Words like 'Colonial', 'Asiatic' and 'Native' were unpopular.[2]

The keepers of empire were clearly shocked about the emerging mood of liberalism. If even black Africans could no longer be publicly discriminated against, what would happen to the remaining vestiges of imperial superiority?

In this political climate the outright condemnation of anti-colonial nationalism had to be tempered with a degree of accommodation. How this was done and with what consequences is the subject of this chapter. Here, the changing focus of Anglo-American interaction with African nationalism is used as a case study to illustrate the wider patterns of Western–Third World relations. It is a story of compromise, which many Western politicians experienced as the appeasement of forces they loathed.

Assumptions of Superiority

In American and British politics African nationalism has always been interpreted as a threatening force. The West spent the interwar years expecting a wave of revenge to sweep Africa. Every manifestation of African autonomy was interpreted as a direct threat to Western interests. Raymond Buell, the most prominent American 'Africanist' of the interwar period, constantly alluded to this expectation in his massive two-volume survey *The Native Problem in Africa*.[3] The approach of African nationalism was widely interpreted as an outburst of frustration against Western rule. The American liberal writer, Louis Snyder, described Pan-Africanism in the 1930s as 'a negative movement brought into being as a result of white penetration into Africa'.[4] In the literature of the next two decades the terms 'unhealthy' and 'frustrated' would often be used to qualify the meaning of African nationalism.

It is important to reiterate the point argued in the last chapter: the strongly held views about the nature of African nationalism were based on no direct experience of this phenomenon. These views actually predate the emergence of African nationalism. As such they confirm the nature of Western attitudes towards the world, rather than revealing anything about the real character of anti-colonial movements. There was very little academic engagement with the subject. Martin Staniland's *American Intellectuals and African Nationalists* argues that until the 1950s, 'American images of the continent were in fact largely shaped by reports furnished by missionaries, explorers, and hunters'.[5] They were also shaped by the intellectual tradition of elitist social theories, as explored in Chapter 3. Indeed until the mid-1950s studies of African political resistance to European domination were conspicuously rare. As late as 1954 *The American Political Science Review* could complain that this was a 'neglected area' and that therefore 'we have been placed in the uncomfortable position of having to formulate opinions and policy and to render judgements without sufficient knowledge'.[6] But ignorance of the subject did not sway Western commentators from their firm convictions about the negative qualities of African nationalism.

African political protest was always interpreted from a perspective informed by assumptions of Western superiority – racial, cultural and moral. It is necessary to recall that until the exposure of the consequences of Nazism, the idea of racial superiority was a respectable one in the Anglo-American intellectual tradition. For example, those colonial administrators in attendance at a 1938 Oxford University summer school would have heard a lecture on race by Professor Le Gros Clark. His argument was that although the mentality of a Kenyan boy compared 'favourably' with that of a European one, by the time he reaches maturity his 'development is for some reason retarded'.[7] However, by the late 1940s such explicitly biologically oriented explanations of race had become less prevalent.

Nevertheless, even in the more egalitarian climate of the 1940s, the assumptions of racial superiority did not disappear. They merely became less explicit or were recast in moral terms. In relation to African nationalism, the argument favoured by many American and British officials was that Africans were not ready – often because they were morally unprepared – for national self-determination. In other words the principle of national self-determination was upheld in the abstract, while its relevance to Africa was denied. This standpoint was clearly expressed by Perry N. Jester, one of the American State Department's most effective diplomats in Africa and the Caribbean in the 1950s. In reply to a request for ideas for the formulation of an African policy, Jester wrote in February 1950:

> The peoples in Black Africa are basically primitive rather than backward, due to racial characteristics and environmental influences. It is not a question of fostering and encouraging economic development and political consciousness, building on some sort of pre-existing foundation. It is a question of finding ways of appropriately introducing to these people, guiding concepts in the fields just named, at an elementary level. The same applies to social, cultural and moral

development. Without the guidance of the European, the great majority of the native peoples in Black Africa would be lost in many elementary day-to-day affairs, let alone the management of a state in the twentieth century.[8]

Jester's view would not have provoked controversy among its audience in the State Department. Indeed, most British and American officials would have agreed with his assessment.

As far as Africa was concerned American diplomats tended to rely on British expertise for insights on what was happening. Despite conflicts over policy, the records show that American officials regularly consulted British colonial administrators and tended to accept what they heard about Africans. Differences existed in evaluating the problem posed by anti-colonial nationalism, but *not* about the nature of the African.

Most British imperial officials had distinctly low expectations of the African. T.K. Lloyd, a leading mandarin at the Colonial Office, believed that African troops 'cannot stand up to the strain of modern warfare unless they are personally led by white officers'. Governor Sir Charles Dundas of Uganda assured Whitehall in March 1943 that 'our African is not yet ready for governance' though one day 'he must grow up'. When the Governor of Nigeria, Sir Arthur Richards, argued against extending the franchise in 1946 on the grounds that Africans were illiterate devotees of cannibalism, witchcraft and mass murder, he was giving only a more vivid version of the case found in other contemporary accounts:

> This is a country where barely 5% of the population can read or write, where for generations the peasant has been far too concerned with the problem of existence to concern himself with anything but the most petty local affairs, where in large areas the natives, men and women, go unclothed, where cannibalism is still practised, where secret societies based on ju-ju can still indulge in mass murder, where the very leaders of organised labour invoke ju-ju to impart discipline.[9]

From this standpoint self-determination made little sense. Africans clearly needed white officers and European guidance. As the Governor of Sierra Leone argued in 1949, his colony which had only just begun to 'emerge from the primitive', was 'in its adolescence and it needs help and guidance', not self-determination.[10]

Others insisted on the essentially depraved character of the African. The British Resident in Buganda wrote in May 1946:

> It must also be remembered that the cloak of civilisation merely covers and does not remove the national characteristics of the Buganda.

Individually and collectively they are still prone to intrigue; they are self ambitious and only concerned with what will advance the interests of the individual: they are crafty, credulous and cruel.[11]

Clearly these people were not worthy of the kind of trust or respect that was due to honest, intrigue-free imperial politicians.

The underlying theme of all these assessments was that the African lacked the moral responsibility necessary for political independence. 'The standard of African public morality is low', was the verdict of one relatively liberal official at Whitehall in 1946.[12] By implication African public figures, not just in Buganda but throughout the continent, were motivated by individual greed rather than any wider political and social concerns.

The condescending dismissal of any lofty motives among Africans existed in a state of tension with the realisation that some anti-Western force was growing in influence and had become a threat to the existing order. Manifestations of political protest and labour disputes in the 1940s seemed to question the image of the childlike African who was unconcerned with wider social affairs. This tension was resolved by the reinterpretation of crowd theory in the African context. According to the new wisdom, the African masses were still living in a stage of adolescence but they could be stirred up and manipulated by malevolent outside forces. From this perspective African nationalism could be accepted as real, but branded as the artificial product of forces *external* to colonial society.

'Instigated largely by subversive movements in New York, Manchester and other places, there is at present an attempt to create a sort of synthetic black nationalism, frequently called Pan Africanism or Africa for the Africans', wrote Governor Philip Mitchell of Kenya in September 1948. This manufactured import to Africa could be manipulated to create mass disorder. Mitchell warned that in 'Africa it is exploited by dangerous and corrupt persons such as Jomo Kenyatta for their personal profit, and it can lead to serious outbreaks'.[13] The scenario drawn up by Mitchell combined the assumptions of elite theory with that of racial superiority. Africans were too 'primitive' to be genuine nationalists but they were also too 'immature' to resist the propaganda of demagogues and subversives. This model was attractive since it allowed outbursts of protest to be explained away as having no indigenous causation in the colonial relationship. Instead, they were caused by external subversion or outside agitation. Communist agents or other subversives became responsible for anti-colonial protest – or at the very least, they became the carriers of the disease of nationalism.

Mitchell's aside about Kenyatta is not incidental. In the Anglo-American image of African protest the educated or 'detribalised' native became the villain of the piece. Often described as 'half-educated' or 'semi-educated' they were portrayed as mobilising the masses for their own selfish ends. Precisely because they were detribalised, they were held to represent no one but themselves. This was the reassuring message of an article in the *Round Table* in 1948: 'the detribalized, educated Westernized native is apt to be as much out of touch and sympathy with his own race as is the European'.[14] The 'so-called' African intelligentsia was also scorned by those committed to reforming the Empire. Thus in 1949 we find W.M. Macmillan, a liberal critic of Empire, holding forth on how 'dangerous a little learning can be' in Africa.[15]

The denunciations of the educated/detribalised African often assumed extreme proportions. They expose a reaction against anybody whose existence seemed to refute racial certainties. Jester's discussion of African leadership is paradigmatic:

There is no widespread development of moral integrity which would lend constancy to their activities and make possible the fulfilment of commitments. There is everywhere ignorance, sloth and petty cupidity. For the most part, those who have received the benefits of higher education abroad return not to uplift, enlighten or ennoble their own people, but rather to exploit them.[16]

This unflattering depiction of the educated African emphasises the moral disintegration of the leaders of anti-colonial protest. Precisely because they are educated they are different – but because they are African they cannot be like their European counterpart. Neither traditional nor modern, these products of maladjustment can only destroy. Once the Cold War starts, the educated African becomes the classical patsy for the communist subversive. A Foreign Office survey of communism in Africa in August 1950 put the argument thus:

The black natives, as might be expected, are more easy to mould than the arabs, and the 'detribalised' blacks the easiest of all … The semi-educated, detribalised native, having lost the moral and social buttress of the rigidly tribal community, tends to fall as easy prey to the Communist agitator.[17]

The educated African exists in a moral vacuum and thus become susceptible to totalitarian influences. In a sense the educated African personified the worse fears of the Anglo-American imagination regarding the nature of anti-colonial protest.

The uprooted African mind is portrayed as the cause of instability. Social instability becomes the product not of colonial rule but of *unstable* minds. The manipulation of these minds creates a disease far worse than that which inflicted the crowds imagined by European theorists of mass society. In these circumstances, nationalism becomes a disease of epidemic proportions. According to a Foreign Office paper:

> Exploited or dissatisfied nationalism produces a state of mind in which any sense of grievance, injustice or inferiority is magnified out of all proportion. This can lead to a state of unbalance amounting in the worse case to hysteria. This state of mind is highly infectious.[18]

The diagnosis of disorder now had a veritable foundation in the medical sciences.

The Pragmatism of Diplomacy

Whatever the prevailing attitude toward African nationalism, policy considerations demanded a degree of accommodation. Precisely because the effects of this force were feared, both British and American officials tried to take precautionary steps. Back in 1937, Lord Hailey had warned against provoking a reaction through 'undue insistence on colour superiority'. His message was the need to interact with the aspiration of Africans in order to neutralise the danger posed by nationalism. 'Thwarted it can be dangerous; met in the right spirit, it can be guided into fruitful and constructive channels', argued Hailey.[19] By the late 1940s this was the policy of the British Colonial Office. The Secretary of State for the Colonies, after observing that the 'emotional fervour attached to nationalism infects and spreads' warned that 'unless a serious effort is made to channel it, it may become disruptive and destructive'.[20]

If anything, American officials were even more pragmatic than the British. Americans initially feared that an unambiguous imperialist reaction to African nationalism would drive it in a general anti-Western reaction. Later the same fear was expressed in relation to the danger of pushing African nationalism towards the wrong side of the Cold War. American intelligence reports on Africa underlined the importance of preparing to meet the challenge of the emerging political movements. One report written in 1944 noted that African nationalism was 'more significant from the point of view of its potentialities than from its past or present strength'.[21]

The expectation of political instability encouraged British and American officials to think in experimental terms. Fearing future threats to imperial rule, officials at the Colonial Office began to evolve policies which would eventually culminate in decolonisation. Throughout the Second World War colonial officials were continually concerned about the disruptive effect returning soldiers would have on colonial society. The American Consul in Accra reported a high level of anxiety in government circles concerning this subject.[22] The need to pre-empt African revolts – the term 'decolonise' was not yet in currency – was strongly advocated by those sensitive to the prevailing political climate in the mid 1940s. Those charged with promoting imperial propaganda often seemed to fear that Britain was running out of time. 'My conclusions are pessimistic' wrote a worried Harold Evans in July 1944: 'However benevolent our policy, however fast we work, it will be neither benevolent enough nor fast enough for the vocal, self-seeking urban African'.[23] Nevertheless the policy of political reform appeared as the best available instrument for preventing nationalism from becoming a destructive force. Of course there were sceptics. At the 1947 Cambridge summer school for colonial officials there was a clear divide between administrators from Africa and bureaucrats from Whitehall. Officials working in Africa feared the consequences of decolonisation.[24]

The Americans were in principle solidly behind decolonisation. If anything, in the immediate aftermath of the Second World War they seemed critical of Britain's slowness in implementing its strategy. American attitudes towards Africa were motivated both by Washington's conflict of interest with its British competitor, and its awareness of its global role as the new premier world power.

America's conflict of interest with Britain in the 1940s was well illustrated in South Africa, where the American representative argued that a victory for the National Party in the coming election could well serve US interests, since the old Smuts Government was too pro-Empire.[25] America's concern with global security also disposed it to question Britain's attitude towards African nationalism. American diplomats often expressed concern that unless Britain responded positively to anti-colonial aspirations, African nationalism would help consolidate anti-Western sentiments and strengthen racial awareness. During the period 1945–7, American officials stationed in Africa tended to be more sensitive to the prevailing political mood than their British counterparts. Thus we find the American Consul in August 1946 in Nairobi complaining that the British authorities seemed unresponsive to the development of African protest:

> An interesting development is occurring. The authorities are fully aware of this; but, it would seem at the date of this writing that the majority appear to ignore evolution seemingly not desiring to acknowledge the fact that the black African of East Africa is changing and has a soul all his own. It would appear that the expanding expression on the part of Africans has not yet been taken seriously. One, on the spot, wonders just how long the governmental authorities will adhere to the apparent present day *laissez faire* policy.[26]

Similar despatches warning of the growing tide of anti-colonial consciousness were also received in Washington from West Africa.[27]

American perceptions of African nationalism were heavily influenced by hostility to the Soviet Union. Even before the outbreak of the Cold War, the State Department tended to assess developments in Africa from the standpoint of its relationship with the Soviet Union. A major policy document, *British Colonies of West Africa*, published in 1946, noted with a hint of a warning that 'it is thought that the eyes of certain of the more vociferous African exponents of early political independence have turned toward the USSR because of what they consider to be the Soviet Union's advanced attitude toward dependent peoples'.[28] With the outbreak of the Cold War, the fear that the Soviet Union would become a beneficiary of anti-colonial struggles in Africa became the dominant theme in the formulation of American policy.

Despite conflicts of national interest and differences of emphasis, British and American policy tended to converge during the period 1948–60. Both parties recognised that African nationalism was a factor that could not be ignored and that would, in any case, become a more potent force in the future. Britain saw this force as a threat to its empire; American saw it as a threat to the outcome of the Cold War and to the overall integrity of the West. The conclusion drawn by both parties was that, through a combination of concessions and the use of coercion, African nationalism could be influenced and its dangerous effects neutralised. This pragmatic outlook coexisted with the previously established intellectual universe which regarded African nationalism intrinsically as a problem. The assumption of moral superiority was also retained.

A close examination of the shifting emphases of Anglo-American diplomacy in Africa from the late 1940s onwards reveals an underlying pattern: an attempt to accommodate the demands of African nationalism without abandoning the old assumptions of Western superiority.

Forced to find new ways in which to contain the threat from the colonies, the Western powers developed a flexible strategy which at times incorporated everything from insincere flattery to outright repression. Throughout all the shifts of emphasis their aim remained to maintain control of African nationalism.

The Management of Nationalism, 1948–60

As the Cold War took off, America's attitude towards anti-colonial resistance became more cautious. As Noer argues, America saw 'rapid independence for Africa and Asia as dangerous to the Western alliance and to the colonial peoples'.[29] American perceptions of events in Africa were directly shaped by the massive upheavals in post-war Asia. The State Department regarded events in North Africa with alarm and feared the creation of another Indochina.[30] Many American officials regarded the Accra riots of 1948 as evidence that communist subversion was rife on the continent. The American Consul in Accra actually believed that the British were for some reason reluctant to publish the information they must possess regarding Soviet subversion. He complained that it 'strikes me as a great mistake for the Government ... to keep the public in ignorance of the facts, no matter what the facts'.[31]

For the British, the American obsession with communism was a welcome development. It helped to ease American pressure on Britain to decolonise. Although in public American politicians would still make anti-colonial speeches, behind the scenes they were in no hurry to rock the boat. Indeed at times the State Department even expressed concern at the speed with which Britain seemed to be decolonising in the Gold Coast.[32] This fear of communism would be used by Britain time and again to gain American support for its actions in Africa.

Towards Decolonisation

Both Britain and the United States regarded the question of African nationalism as above all a problem of control. Even those who claimed to be sympathetic to the 'advance' of colonial peoples were convinced that African protest was driven by frustration and anger rather then mature reflection. Because of the challenge it represented to the existing order it was intrinsically a law and order problem. This was particularly the view of British officials, since they were the ones most involved in maintaining order.

The issue of imperial control was uppermost in the mind of Arthur Creech-Jones, the reforming Secretary of State for the Colonies. A month before the outbreak of the 1948 Accra Riots, Creech-Jones undertook to deal 'firmly' with African nationalists. He wrote:

there are incipient nationalist movements in Nigeria and Kenya. These may well be a danger to the development of the territories concerned and I agree entirely that our policy with regard to them must be firm and resolute.[33]

Creech-Jones had no specific danger in mind. The need to be 'firm and resolute', appeared as a self-evident response to any challenge to the imperial order.

Creech-Jones understood that Britain lacked the means to satisfy the social and political aspiration of African people. 'The increasing awareness of the colonial people and our failure to give them all the satisfaction they want make them an easy prey to subversive influences', he wrote in October 1948.[34] Not everyone was able to adopt his objective, almost detached point of view. The reaction of many colonial officials to outbursts of anti-colonial protest was often one of anxious incomprehension. Kenneth Bradley's reaction to the Accra riots typified the response of many officials on the ground. For Bradley, soon to become head of the public relations department of the Colonial Office, this outburst was about 'looting and burning in a wild orgy of anarchy and greed'. He concluded that the 'veneer of civilisation seemed to have been stripped off and what lay underneath looked very ugly'.[35]

An uneasy tension existed between the relatively balanced assessment of a Creech-Jones and the tendency to demonise African nationalism on the part of many colonial administrators. But regardless of the view adopted, all sides agreed that nationalism was potentially dangerous. As one official argued in July 1952, nationalism 'if allowed to continue unchecked in its present influence in international politics, will lead to the disintegration of our position in the world'.[36] From this perspective evolved an emphasis on firm control.

For Britain there was no inconsistency between the politics of force and the politics of decolonisation. A forceful approach was required to retain existing interests. The guiding of nationalism gradually emerged as the dominant policy response to anti-colonial protest. But guidance required periodic displays of repression against those who would not be moved, and the support of those who would. Britain had no ambitious blueprint about how decolonisation would proceed. It was seen as a way of giving Britain enough time to influence African nationalists. The idea was to isolate the extremists and help consolidate the position of moderate African politicians.[37] Once nationalists had accepted the rules of the game established by Britain and were insulated from mass pressure, decolonisation could proceed.

Gaining time to influence African nationalism was critical for Britain. The Colonial Office regarded its experiment of guiding the nationalist movement in the Gold Coast as something of a model. 'Arden Clarke is hopeful', wrote one senior Colonial Office mandarin about the Governor of the Gold Coast, that 'he can spin out the next stage of constitutional change over a period of perhaps some 18 months'.[38]

The policy of decolonisation did not imply a revision of the British view of African nationalism. The consensus was that African nationalism was still an immature movement, but a dangerous one that had to be met with guile and not just with force. The policy was to guide it rather than just fight it. In Nigeria this policy implied the simultaneous cultivation of individual nationalist leaders and the repression of the radical Zikists. This combination of judicious manipulation of nationalist politicians, constitutional reform and selective repression allowed Britain to gain time. As the Governor of Nigeria, Sir John Macpherson, later recalled:

> In west Africa we granted constitutional advance at a pace beyond the true competence of the people, but this was a calculated risk taken to avoid a cataclysm if we had failed to carry the young educated people with us and had tried to depend solely upon traditional authorities and 'uncle Toms'.[39]

The idea was to manage African nationalism by staying ahead, encouraging collaborators and retaining the initiative.

During this period, American policy towards African nationalism tended to be rather weak and incoherent. Possibly the State Department was too distracted by its other concerns to pay much attention to Africa. It was only in 1950 that the State Department established its office of African Affairs under the directorship of Elmer H. Bourgerie. George McGhee, the Assistant Secretary of State of the time, retrospectively conceded that there was 'no comprehensive US policy' for Africa.[40] The overriding policy consideration for Washington was how to keep Africa within the 'Free World'.

Formally, America adopted a middle position of supporting 'legitimate' anti-colonial protest while upholding an orderly form of change. Washington was faced with the dilemma that its close allies were also the targets of African nationalism. As Bourgerie argued:

We must never forget that the anti-colonial feeling in certain African territories constitutes a formidable problem for the Free World because all of the Colonial Governments are aligned on the side of the Free World. Such a condition facilitates rather than militates against Soviet encroachment.[41]

In practice this tension was resolved by placing Cold War considerations to the fore. From 1950 onwards this meant giving the defeat of communism a priority over the aspirations of African nationalism. In June 1950, McGhee warned about the danger of 'premature independence for primitive, underdeveloped peoples' who would be unable to counter subversion and hence would threaten the 'security of the free world'.[42]

From time to time American diplomats drew attention to the 'ticklish Britain versus nationalist dichotomy'.[43] American diplomats stationed in Africa were concerned that if they appeared to be too neutral then they could lose influence with anti-colonial nationalists. By 1950 some American diplomats were also concerned to counter the impression that the USA's own record on race was open to criticism by Africans. Calls for public relations material on race relations within the United States indicated that officials were becoming sensitised to the problem of dealing with African political aspirations.[44]

In practice the State Department was prepared to rely on Britain to handle political agitation in the colonies. This was to some extent a pragmatic policy since Britain would take the anti-colonial flak. It also indicated that Washington had no substantive disagreement with British policy in Africa. Despite the formal adherence of the United States to political advance and decolonisation, it was far more concerned to stop Britain moving too fast to change things.

Although the State Department relied to a considerable extent on British assessments of African nationalism, it often expressed misgivings about Whitehall's zeal for reform. There seemed to be a sneaking suspicion in Washington that Britain may well have underestimated the danger of communist subversion posed by African nationalism. At a joint meeting held at the Foreign Office of American and British officials this was the underlying theme of the discussion.[45]

The State Department's fear that Britain was perhaps moving too fast indicated that it had less confidence in the project of guiding and controlling African nationalism. A despatch from the American Consul in Accra in November 1951 expresses the widespread scepticism regarding the viability of decolonisation that prevailed in the State Department:

In essence what is happening here is this. A rapidly increasing measure of self-government is being given to an African people who, in the first place are not really threatening to take it by force; and to a people who, on the whole, are very vague about what it is and may not even be too enthusiastic about getting it. It is being given to a people who have no natural unity ... who remain largely illiterate and uneducated, whose economy is underdeveloped and seriously unbalanced – in short, who began to come out of the jungle, figuratively and to some extent literally speaking, only two or three generations ago, and who are not ready to manage their own affairs in a modern society by any standards which heretofore have been considered reasonable.[46]

The argument was that Africans were not yet ready for independence and that Britain was taking a risk in its plans for the Gold Coast. At this point the main contribution of the State Department to the policy of decolonisation was its ceaseless demand that radicals and communists should be marginalised in Gold Coast politics.

American diplomacy was much too pessimistic. Britain's policy of decolonisation helped to minimise the danger of unrest. That decolonisation coincided with the deradicalisation of anti-colonial protest is no coincidence. British policy was relatively successful in isolating radical opponents.[47] For example, in 1953 the Colonial Office successfully prevailed on Nkrumah to purge the so-called extremists inside his movement. Extending the era of decolonisation also worked in Britain's favour. The prospect of independence led to the escalation of divisions inside the different nationalist movements. These divisions, which often acquired a regional or ethnic expression, helped to weaken Britain's opponents. Typically, Gorell Barnes, head of the Africa Desk at the Colonial Office was counting on 'inter-tribal jealousy and suspicion' to 'act as a curb on extreme African nationalism' in Kenya.[48]

Repression and ethnic manipulation were obvious instruments used by Britain to manage African nationalism. But these measures were only the means to capturing African nationalist movements. Most important of all was the attempt by Britain to shape African nationalism itself. The success of this policy was illustrated by the ability to transfer power to relatively moderate African governments from the Gold Coast to Kenya.

A Changing Division of Labour

During the second half of the 1950s the difference in emphasis between Britain and America regarding the threat of African nationalism became more pronounced. Possibly this was due to American concern about Soviet success in the Third World and British complacency regarding the success of its policy in Africa.

In substance the views of Britain and America regarding Africans and their nationalism had changed very little. Whatever African nationalism was, ran the argument, it had little to do with the qualities possessed by European nationalism. According to a 1950 Foreign Office study, the term nationalism was 'misleading since, in most of the African continent, the concept of a nation is as yet unknown' and added that term nationalism was used for 'want of a better'.[49] Lord Hailey's revised 1956 *African Survey* preferred the term 'Africanism' to 'nationalism'. According to Hailey, the 'movement of Africanism has so far shown little coherence'.[50] In most British official studies in the 1950s it is difficult to find any positive characteristics associated with African nationalism. The adjectives used to describe it are 'unhealthy', 'frustrated', 'extreme', etc. Probably the best thing that Whitehall could say about African nationalism was that it was not as bad as communism.

A 1953 study commissioned by the Colonial Office warned that the 'wrong kind of nationalism' was developing. It noted that since 'ambitions so far outrun immediate possibilities, frustration grows and with it envy, hatred and malice and all uncharitableness'. And yet the same report is not at all unconfident about future prospects. It notes the absence of 'any hatred of Britain'. The author Harold Ingrams is reasonably certain that a sophisticated policy of decolonisation could protect Britain's interests.[51]

It appears that although the Colonial Office still regarded Africans as unsuited to run their affairs and was concerned that Soviet subversives could gain influence among the naive masses, it also believed that it remained in control of the situation. This view of Africa was less and less shared by Washington. Haunted by the success of nationalist movements in Asia and the Middle East, the USA expected a rerun in Africa. The presentiment of disorder which had been prevalent in the West for decades was fleshed out by foreign policy setbacks in Asia.

Africa: a Special Assessment, expressed the State Department mood in early 1956. This major report was far more downbeat about future prospects than its British counterpart. 'So potentially explosive are the elements compounded in present-day Africa', it argued, 'that outbreaks of violence will be inevitable during the next decade'. The report expected insurrection in North Africa and explosions of violence in Libya, Sudan and the Gold Coast. Growing disorder was also predicted in Kenya and South Africa.[52]

As far as perceptions of African nationalism are concerned, there was little difference between the two Western powers. The relevant officials of both powers were convinced that Africans were not ready for independence. When the American Consul in Nairobi wrote in 1955 that 'unfortunately, the capacity of the Africans for self-government is not matching the increasing tempo of the nationalist movement', he was echoing the views of the local administration.[53] The difference between the Americans and the British was in the assessment of how big a problem African nationalism posed. As far as Washington was concerned, Britain was clearly underestimating the danger.

The difference in the assessment of African nationalism was due not simply to varying degrees of confidence. By the mid 1950s Americans began to realise that sooner or later Britain would withdraw from the continent. Likewise, Britain was concerned with rationalising its relationship with Africa. From 1955–6 onwards the American State Department began to assume an increasingly independent stance towards Africa. It was as if it assumed that soon it would have to bear the burden of managing African nationalism.

In many British colonies in Africa, the United States was stepping up its activity, initiating contacts with local politicians and working out contingency plans in case Britain failed to maintain order. For example, during the Mau Mau emergency the American Consul in Nairobi proposed a five-point programme for raising his country's profile in East Africa. He warned that Pax Britannica alone could not indefinitely guarantee order in the region:

> If in East Africa we are to avoid the catastrophe of China and the rampant extremism of some parts of the Middle East, we should start to develop contacts whenever and wherever we can and we should then build upon the foundations we lay.[54]

This attitude was shared in Washington. During the years that followed there was a major escalation of American diplomatic activity.

Americans were buying influence and the British predictably reacted with resentment. The rivalries which were to some extent suspended in the late 1940s and early 1950s became more pronounced from 1956–7 onwards. The Suez crisis enhanced the sense of British isolation. From this period there is a constant stream of complaints about how American policy was serving to undermine British efforts in Africa.[55] Although it is difficult to quantify from the available evidence, it seems that British officials were far more preoccupied with the activities of their American rivals than the Americans were with them.

Flattering Nationalism

Despite the escalation of American diplomatic activity, Britain continued to take the initiative in relation to African nationalism. The major policy innovation of Whitehall during the mid 1950s towards Africa was its policy of flattering nationalism. This was an entirely pragmatic policy which cynically attempted to project Britain as the friend of African nationalism. The new approach was possible because African nationalist movements had become contained and to some extent institutionalised. Flattering nationalism was a policy designed to win Britain goodwill in its twilight years in Africa.

As independence became more and more of a reality, Whitehall became anxious to consolidate relationships with the African political elite. The art of diplomacy assumed a new importance and it was thought important to avoid publicly offending African sensibilities. In any case leading officials in the Colonial and Foreign Offices became convinced that within the context of the Cold War, African nationalism need not be a problem. Many regarded African nationalism as a potential bulwark against communism and other radical influences. The view was that African nationalism was a reality; it would not go away and therefore it was better to live with it than to fight it. Moreover, many British officials believed on the basis of their previous experience of managing nationalism that it could be used as a resource in the Cold War.

One symptom of changing attitudes to African nationalism was the relatively positive reaction in Whitehall to the phenomenon of Pan-Africanism. Whitehall looked upon Nkrumah's calling of a Pan-African conference in 1957 benignly. At the very least it represented a 'challenge to Egypt's claims to leadership of the continent' and, argued the Foreign Office, it 'should be all to the good' for Britain.[56] Even the conservative *Daily Telegraph* welcomed the conference and speculated that it would enhance 'Nkrumah's value to future Commonwealth conferences if he can act as spokesman for a body of African opinion'.[57]

During the next two years Britain's belief in its ability to benefit from Pan-Africanism grew. The view of the Foreign Office was that 'we can make positive use of the movement to woo Africans away from both Moscow and Cairo'.[58] This proactive approach towards Pan Africanism was paralleled by a coherent argument for a positive approach to African nationalism, as outlined in a document published by the Foreign Office in November 1958.

The pragmatism of this document, *The Political Scene in Tropical Africa* is striking. Privately Britain's attitude to African nationalism was one

of barely concealed contempt. But publicly the British were prepared
to praise it. In effect they were flattering or patronising African nationalism. 'It is perfectly true that Africans have none of the glorious history
which is such an inspiration to the Arabs and no background of unity',
observed the authors of this document. However there was little point
in dwelling on this because 'educated Africans are acutely sensitive to
colour'. In any case the future growth of this movement was considered
inevitable and therefore it 'would be a serious mistake on the part of
the West to underestimate, or to try to repress, the tide of what Lord
Hailey aptly calls "Africanism"'.

The document counsels indulgence towards the activities of Pan-
Africanists. It calls for the sensitive handling of what it portrays as
insecure individuals who will cling to any symbol that strengthens their
African identity. The authors note:

> This process will call for great self-restraint on the part of the mother
> countries, the more so since the foreign policy of young and inex-
> perienced nations is apt to be erratic. Children like to form their own
> friendships and to be members of groups of their own contempo-
> raries; nevertheless they are unlikely to choose the complete rupture
> of the family ties so long as they feel they have the confidence and
> respect of their parents.

This classic statement of imperial paternalism was based on the view
that Britain could at least neutralise African nationalism. That is why it
suggested that 'Pan-africanism may provide a strong natural defence against
Soviet and Egyptian influences'.[59]

In passing it should be noted that a close reading of this document
suggests that its sense of confidence was self-consciously inflated. The
frequent repetition of metaphors that connote African inferiority looks
more like an exercise in self-persuasion than a symptom of certainty
on Britain's part.

The approach of the United States to African nationalism was lagging
behind that of Britain. To be sure it was stepping up its diplomatic
presence, consolidating contacts and providing scholarships to aspiring
African intellectuals. The United States Information Service (USIS) was
expressly using American blacks to front many of the cultural and social
initiatives. American power, wealth and prestige proved important
resources in establishing a degree of collaboration with many African
nationalists.

However American policy was less flexible then that of Britain.
Washington was deeply suspicious of neutralism, non-alignment and

initially of Pan-Africanism. President Eisenhower looked upon the arrival of African independence as a 'destructive hurricane'. 'Premature independence and irresponsible nationalism may present grave dangers to dependent peoples' was the verdict of assistant Secretary of State C. Burke Elbrick in his statement to the Senate Foreign Relations Committee in 1958.[60]

The Eisenhower administration feared that African nationalists would naturally align themselves with the Soviet Union. The policy of supporting or co-operating neutral or Third Worldist perspectives had few adherents in the State Department. Back in 1954, the US scholar Robert Scalapino wrote that 'many Americans view "neutralism" as a new type of social disease'.[61] This sentiment was not without influence in Washington in the late 1950s.

Initially State Department officials were sceptical of British initiatives designed to flatter African nationalism. Officials at Whitehall were sensitive to American disapproval. However, the apparent success of the British strategy led to a reorientation towards a more positive approach to African nationalism. By early 1958 the State Department was patronising the concept of 'African personality'. Its briefing on the impending Pan-African Conference at Accra hoped 'that the Accra Conference can in the main result in some moderate statements and declarations that will serve in the aggregate to balance the recent Soviet-Egyptian circus in Cairo'. It added that it was 'of course, probable that the Conference will inevitably produce some racial, anti-colonial and neutralist heat'.[62] One official at Whitehall cynically remarked that if the Americans get carried away with flattering the 'African Personality', it 'might produce embarrassing results'.[63]

The State Department seemed to adopt the new policy of cultivating African nationalism with gusto. Pointing to the new approach as it first manifested itself to the 1958 Accra Conference, one British diplomat wrote that 'the Americans are for once taking a less cautious line than ourselves'.[64] Americans were pleasantly surprised that their new policy could win them diplomatic advantage and a few friends.

A Legacy of Moral Uncertainties

The expectation of disorder which preceded the emergence of mass political movement in Africa remained part of the Anglo-American mental universe. The pragmatic policy which had evolved appeared to minimise the destruction which African nationalism could be expected to cause. But although the policy appeared to work it was not without its cost. By eventually accepting the legitimacy of African nationalism, Anglo-American assumptions of superiority were put to question. For a while it even appeared to many that it was the Third World which held the high ground. Moreover if African nationalism was now held to be legitimate, it retrospectively called into question the moral authority of colonial rule.

Flattering African nationalism did not come easily. The resentment of having to abandon the certainty that came with a firm sense of superiority is evident in the writings of both American and British officials. Even at the height of the promotion of this policy there was a tendency to denounce African nationalism as morally inferior to that of the West. For example, a British diplomat in Leopoldville reported the killing of 200 people in Brazzaville 'where a black African Government under Abbe Youlou is in control'. He added:

> Yet, so far as I am aware, public opinion has been unmoved; we are all too polite even to protest. When anything goes wrong in a colonial territory we all begin to flagellate ourselves; but what Africans do to Africans is nobody's business.[65]

Here was an argument which would become standard in succeeding decades. The argument against appeasing African nationalism was at once a retrospective defence of colonial rule. From this standpoint the problem was that of guilty liberals who were oblivious to the destructive character of African nationalism and to the positive contribution of colonialism.

The resentment expressed above was also fuelled by the sense that moral authority was somehow slipping away from the West. Suddenly the whole tradition of imperial glory appeared shabby and unconvincing. The arguments in defence of Empire lacked conviction. Lord Winster, for example, sounded positively defensive when he insisted that 'we have no need to be ashamed of our colonial record'.[66] The sheer number of calls insisting that there was no need to be ashamed exposed the insecurity of the British establishment.

By the late 1950s the British Government was aware that it was losing its influence over Africa. Harold Macmillan, the Prime Minister, hardly sounded like a confident imperial master when he asked for ideas as to how to retain influence in Africa. His own suggestion, that more 'thought ought to be given to the role of Christianity in keeping the Africans oriented towards Western ideals' indicated the paucity of options available for Britain.[67] The very discussion around Macmillan's proposal revealed that the British establishment had ceased to believe in its imperial mission. Resentment at having to give way to the morally inferior African nationalist was now combined with a sense of demoralisation about the tangible loss of influence.

Then the Congo exploded in 1960. It seemed to confirm all the worst fears of the State Department. With the internationalisation of the conflict and the possibility of Soviet intervention there appeared the danger of losing Africa in the Cold War. But the Congo also served as proof that in African nationalism, civilisation faced a terrible danger. All the old anxieties about primitive and atavistic terror were confirmed. Father John Dean's account of the horror was typical of the press stories of the time:

> I couldn't recognise the sisters, although I had worked with them for eight months. Their veils had been ripped off, their clothes torn. Their hair was all wild. One had been so abused she had to be carried ... We were beaten all the way and villagers shrieked 'White men you are going to die' ... The women were lined up and one by one the Africans, all crazed by drink, assaulted them.[68]

The Congo experience helped reinforce the underlying perceptions about African savagery, even while the policy of flattering African nationalism was proceeding. It did not resolve the moral uncertainty of the Anglo-American imagination, but it did at least limit the damage done to their worldview by pursuing a pragmatic course. The Western response to events in the Congo also indicated how the failures associated with African nationalism in the future would contribute to the moral rearmament of the imperial mind.

5 Imperialism on the Defensive: the Campaign to Limit the Damage

Most studies of decolonisation stress the changing balance of power between coloniser and colonised. One important theme in this drama has been unfortunately neglected: the setback that decolonisation represented to the self-image of imperialism. The assumptions of superiority and of mission and moral authority have always been important to the self-esteem of the Anglo-American elite. To a considerable extent, it was the culture of imperialism which gave this elite a sense of coherence as a political force. It follows that once this culture was put to question – practically, ideologically and intellectually – it undermined the moral pretensions of the elite.

The strong Western reaction to the rise of Third World nationalism can be explained in part as a recognition that the imperial political culture could not survive in its existing form. Anti-colonial resistance was not merely a claim for power but also for legitimacy. In so far as this claim met with success it was experienced as the negation of Western authority. The phenomenon generally described as the rise of the Third World was therefore invariably treated with suspicion in the West.

However, the climate that prevailed in the 1940s was inhospitable to the traditional culture of imperialism. The events of the Second World War created a strong reaction against imperialism and colonialism in the West, which predictably encouraged nationalist forces in the colonies to become more assertive. This response – and in particular the anti-colonial revolts in Asia – dealt a death blow to the European empires. The Soviet Union also contributed to imperial woes. The rise of the Soviet Union to the status of a major global power limited the West's room for manoeuvre in the Third World. Officials in London and Washington sensed that dissatisfied colonial politicians could turn to Moscow and expect a degree of support. Soviet competition forced the Western powers to go further then they would have liked in accommodating to anti-colonial nationalism.

The accommodation the West made to anti-colonial nationalism, partly in response to the demands of the Cold War, was intensely resented by the political elites. As far as they were concerned they were now forced in public to treat as equals representatives of societies that they clearly considered to be their inferiors. The Anglo-American elite also found it offensive that the Third World should claim the moral high ground. A former editor of the American *National Review* commented that 'lacking material force, the Bandung nations fall back upon "morality" because there is no other road open to them'.[1]

This is why many in the West reserved a special hatred for the United Nations. Criticism from the UN delegates of recently independent states, who sometimes outvoted their former colonial masters, provoked strong emotions in the West. The sense of revulsion is palpable in former British Prime Minister Harold Macmillan's reaction to this state of affairs. Macmillan bemoaned the 'loss of white prestige' before blaming the ideological competition of the Cold War because 'it puts a tremendous blackmailing weapon into the hands of quite unimportant countries in the Afro-Asian camp who, if it were not for the tremendous rivalry between Russia and the Free World, would not be able to sell their favours so dear'.[2]

The forced accommodation to anti-colonial nationalism did not mean merely a sense of defensiveness in the here and now. It also called into question the imperialist tradition and culture of the past. A lot was at stake in terms of elite self-confidence and legitimacy. Accommodation to anti-colonial nationalism meant nothing less than that the *Western political elite had been forced to deny itself*. How the officials and intellectuals of this elite coped with this problem is the subject of this chapter.

The Imperial Ideal in Retreat

It is easy to forget that until the 1930s the moral claims of imperialism were seldom questioned in the West. Imperialism and the global expansion of the Western powers were represented in unambiguously positive terms as a major contribution to human civilisation. Until the late 1920s individual representatives of the Anglo-American ruling class would often positively define themselves as imperialist. To be an imperialist was considered a respectable political badge. Far from being a source of embarrassment, imperialism and its tradition provided inspiration and confidence to the ruling elites. Even British socialists and liberals were selective in their criticism of imperialism. Taylor is to the point when he states that 'liberals and socialists did not object to British imperialism *per se*, but to the particular aggressive form which it was perceived to take after the Jameson raid of 1895'.[3]

As late as 1949, the future British Labour Prime Minister Harold Wilson could argue that 'no party can or should claim for itself the exclusive use of the title Imperialist, in the best sense of the word'.[4] For Wilson imperialism was a national tradition, 'in the best sense of the word'; it was above question and above party politics. However, by the 1940s this type of reaction was out of time and exceptional. As a result of the experience of the Second World War, imperialism had become widely discredited. Instead of basking in the glory associated with high-minded morality, imperialism had become in many quarters a term of abuse.

The shift of emphasis in the usage of the term imperialism in school textbooks is particularly striking. According to one account of education in the United States, there was a perceptible shift in the 1940s:

> the word 'imperialism', which was once freely used to describe United States adventures in Asia and the Caribbean at the end of the nineteenth century no longer applies to the United States. According to these books, imperialism is a European affair.[5]

This was not an option for a European colonial power like Britain. Its treatment of the subject of imperialism was fraught with far more difficulties than those which faced America.

The imperial ideal first came under serious questioning in the aftermath of the First World War. Lenin's association of imperialism with the drive to war found a widespread public resonance in Europe. At the same time, the escalation of anti-colonial revolts in Asia and the Middle East put to question the moral claims of imperialism. Left-wing opinion in Europe and liberal opinion in the United States were gradually turning against imperialism.

Already on the defensive, imperialists were thrown into disarray by the experience of the Second World War. The war appeared to confirm Lenin's linkage of imperialism and military conflict. The experience of German imperialism under Hitler finally discredited all forms of imperialism. British imperialism, with all of its longstanding assumptions of racial and cultural superiority, faced the problem of guilt by association. These were issues that preoccupied the British establishment from the mid 1930s onwards. Although most of the deliberation on the subject took place in private, on occasion it would enter the public domain.

Although the British establishment succeeded in winning the propaganda battle against Germany, and heaping all of the blame for the war on to Hitler, it could not save the reputation of imperialism. Imperialism and colonialism were no longer accepted as positive or even as neutral terms. After the Nazi experience they acquired an essentially negative connotation in most parts of the world. From time to time British propagandists attempted to retrieve the situation by making an intellectual distinction between good and bad forms of imperialism and colonialism – which often meant British and German colonialism respectively.

It took some time for the British establishment to comprehend the depth and the breath of the reaction to imperialism. In June 1948 one propagandist in the Foreign Office informed his counterpart in the Colonial Office that the 'feeling that to possess colonies is *per se* immoral or, at the very least, incompatible with twentieth century ideas' is a point 'so important as to overshadow the rest'.[6] The discovery that imperialism was immoral took some time to sink in. Almost a decade later a former colonial governor noted in quiet disbelief that 'there are those who believe that any form "colonialism" is inherently evil'.[7] The discrediting of imperialism strongly disoriented the British ruling class. The imperial ideal with its sense of moral purpose had played a critical role in providing the establishment with confidence and coherence. The imperial past had served an important function in legitimising the role of the British ruling class. The new, negative sentiments associated with imperialism strongly undermined the use of the British past as a source of inspiration and authority.

From the late 1940s onwards there a tone of moral defensiveness and of insecurity is discernible in the reactions of Whitehall officials to imperial matters. These reactions were seldom articulated in a systematic form. They generally took the character of unguarded comments and asides.

One symptom of imperial defensiveness were the habitual calls made by imperial publicists and officials against feeling *unconfident*, *guilty*, or *ashamed*. Throughout the 1940s and 1950s articles and books written from the Empire point of view continually reiterate this point. One former colonial officer in Nigeria pointed to the emerging political movements in Africa in 1947 and warned that 'their nationalism will thrive on our fear' and 'our own lack of self confidence'. The former Governor of the Gold Coast, Sir Alan Burns, remarked that 'we are, indeed beginning to be a little ashamed of our position as a colonial Power and inclined to pay undue attention to the self-righteous attitude of other nations'. Professor Vincent Harlow, imperial historian and with close connection to Whitehall wrote about the unfortunate effects – 'almost pathological' – of 'so many in the West' who 'still suffer from a "sense of guilt" about imperialism'.[8]

Those who denounced the faint hearted for feeling shame about the Empire were in a roundabout way saying that the imperial record was beyond reproach. Their argument also implied that the real problem facing the Empire was not the strength of opposition among colonial peoples but the lack of confidence in the imperial ideal within Britain. In a sense those who sought to defend the Empire tried to blame the guilty liberals and the weak-willed in Britain for the prevailing climate of anti-colonialism. In reality even the fiercest defenders of Britain's imperial traditions were not entirely immune from this climate. It became less and less plausible to defend the Empire through the old imperialist rhetoric. But the substitution of the term Commonwealth for Empire did not make much difference.

Some members of the establishment concluded that doubts about the imperial tradition were calling into question the fundamentals of the British way of life. Macmillan's call to the Cabinet in 1952 for a 'march to the Third British Empire' was based on this assumption:

> We are faced at home with a steady intensification of class divisions and that sense of frustration which leads to the rejection of all established institutions; we may have to face at the same time the break-up of the Commonwealth and our decline into a second-rate Power. I see no escape from these dangers except by the fearless proclamation of a policy which will inspire the masses and restore their pride and confidence.[9]

But the time for reasserting pride and confidence through upholding the imperial vision had already passed. Macmillan himself became involved in the winding up of the Empire. And as we noted earlier, Macmillan's own lack of an imperial vision was revealed by his thoughts on how to maintain Britain's role in Africa in the late 1950s. The absence of a strategy for imperial success is obvious in his proposal to use Christianity somehow to retain influence in Africa.

The demoralised tone of Macmillan's proposal expressed the reaction of an elite aware that the consequences of imperial decline were likely to be far-reaching for their way of life. But although they were incapable of generating a positive imperial alternative, the defenders of the Empire were engaged in a rearguard action designed to limit the damage. That they succeeded to an extent is indicated by the fact that most expressions of moral crisis regarding the Empire were contained within establishment circles, and never became issues in the public domain.

Fighting a Rearguard Action

Whitehall was clearly aware that the Empire had become a major problem. International criticism of the British Empire during the Second

World War was a continuous source of anxiety in London. A committee established to monitor American opinion and the British Empire concluded that the 'Colonial Empire was still itself a powerful barrier to understanding between Britain and America'.[10] The international image of the Empire in the postwar period was not a positive one. Criticism of the Empire created a sense of siege in London. A Foreign Office memorandum took the view that 'propaganda against Britain as an Imperial power is being produced from nearly every great power, either by the Government or by interested groups'.[11]

The policy of granting independence to India did not enhance the reputation of the British Empire in Asia. 'Unfortunately others have long memories which the Russians and the Americans keep alive by rubbing in the unpleasantness of not being master in your own home', commented a Foreign Office specialist on Asia.[12] British diplomats from the Middle East concurred, reporting that British propaganda campaigns about the granting of independence to India and Pakistan 'do not carry a great deal of weight'.[13] British publicists were acutely aware of the difficulty of projecting a positive image for the Empire. Information officers stationed in South America, the Middle East and Asia often requested that 'colonial material' should not be sent to them and preferred to avoid the subject altogether.[14] Propagandists suggested that whenever possible imperial themes should be dropped. Information officers in India felt most comfortable with the theme of 'Britain as a political and Social Democracy'. It was suggested that this was the theme 'most easily handled'.[15]

But of course the issue of Empire could not be avoided. Plans drawn up to promote the Empire were self-consciously designed to distance the Commonwealth from the charge of imperialism and exploitation. A report drawn up by the Empire Publicity Sub Committee in February 1944 advanced the following propaganda themes:

> Britain is the centre of world-wide community … It is not imperialistic either in the sense that its parts are exploited, or that it desires territorial expansion.
>
> The Colonial Empire is not Britain's private preserve. Capital investment and trade are not reserved for Britain … The loyalty of the colonial peoples during the war, when their contribution reached remarkable proportions, and their faith in the British connexion, indicate the value and success of the work Britain is doing.[16]

Such propaganda themes were a form of self-flattery which was unlikely to be effective in countering anti-imperialist sentiments outside Britain.

Although Whitehall publicists could do little to alter the overall climate of international opinion, they could attempt to vindicate the Empire by presenting its tradition and policies as fully consistent with the prevailing norms of democracy and self-determination. From the late 1930s, Whitehall officials were involved in a battle of ideas over the record and role of the Empire. The Ministry of Information and the Colonial Office in particular mobilised academic specialists and journalists to join battle. Individuals were approached to write books on imperial subjects. Lecture tours were organised, usually through the British Council. In 1943 the Colonial Office was busy drawing up a shortlist of individuals it would promote in connection with a proposal to establish a chair in colonial history at an American university.[17] Individuals like the historians Vincent Harlow and Nicholas Mansergh were active in public relations, in the Ministry of Information and the Dominion Office respectively.

Whitehall propagandists often approached academics to write books in defence of Empire. One wrote to Lord Elton:

> We feel that this book is so important and the audience which it will reach so large and widespread that it is most urgent for it to be written soon by an authoritative writer. The Colonial Office feels that the book is very badly needed and that no time should be lost in preparing it.[18]

Although this book was not to be written, a lot of other officially inspired ones were. The Ministry of Information helped publish Lord Hailey's *Britain and her Dependencies* and Sir Alfred Zimmern's *From the British Empire to the British Commonwealth*. Other books which received assistance were Vincent Harlow's *The British Colonies* (1944), N. Sabine's, *The British Colonial Empire* (1943), Lucy Mair's, *Welfare in the British Colonies* (1944), Kenneth Bradley's, *Diary of a District Officer* (1943) and W.K. Hancock's, *Argument of Empire* (1943).[19]

Whitehall propagandists were concerned that the intellectual defence of the Empire should be conducted by 'unofficial' sources. The British Council was given the appearance of autonomy from government since 'its work is likely to be done more effectively if it is done not by officials but by persons more closely in touch with the academic world'.[20] In this way the legitimacy of Empire could be expressed through 'independent', 'detached' and 'scholarly' opinion.

The tasks facing the intellectuals of Empire were considerable. Most of the principles associated with the imperialist standpoint stood discredited. The main problem facing imperial intellectuals was that in the 1940s all forms of colonialism were put to question. The linkage between colonialism and oppression deprived Whitehall of the possibility of projecting a plausible policy of progressive colonialism. This was an issue of central concern to Whitehall propagandists. A memorandum by one of the leading propagandists in the Foreign Office, A.A. Dudley, warned that international public opinion no longer tolerated any form of colonialism.[21] It was this notion of colonialism being incompatible with postwar ideas that needed to be challenged.

Arguments on Empire

Various arguments were developed to vindicate the Empire. Some took on board criticisms made of imperialism, others were less flexible and refused to make any concessions to the mood of the time. Former Governor of Kenya, Sir Philip Mitchell's defence of Empire in 1955 was as unyielding as ever:

> I am well aware that 'colonialism' has in our day become a term of reproach, even of abuse; but as a 'colonialist' for forty years ... I am unrepentant and undismayed, although at times fearful lest the current mood of the West should result in 'colonialism' being prematurely abandoned. The process now called 'colonialism' have been, beyond question, the most beneficent, disinterested, and effective force which has ever been brought to bear on Africa in all its history.[22]

Although most arguments were far more diplomatic they shared Mitchell's assumption that in essence the Empire was and remained a force for progress.

Some defenders of Empire, especially imperial historians, argued that British expansion had always contained the progressive impulse of extending freedom and liberty. From this perspective the United Nations-style concepts of partnership and development could be relocated to the colonial past. According to Harlow, the Empire was driven by an essentially moral imperative:

> Of her own initiative Britain has undertaken the task of guiding and training 63 million people of every colour and in every conceivable stage of development, down to the most primitive, in the management of their own affairs.

Harlow suggests that Britain engaged in this worthy enterprise because it benefited everyone.[23]

One approach adopted by the defenders of Empire was to accept that some wrongs had been committed in the past but that the situation had now been rectified. H.V. Hodson, one of the leading propagandists in Whitehall, celebrated a new 'civic conscience' and 'new impulses' which 'have animated British ideas in imperial affairs'.[24] Lord Hailey informed his audience at Princeton University that the 'motives which inspired acquisition of dependencies in the past are not necessarily the same as those which determine the policy followed in their administration today'. Such concessions usually served as a prelude to the argument that a few imperial mistakes paled into insignificance in relation to Britain's positive contribution. Hailey's lecture offers a useful illustration:

> Judged by the standards of today, the past history of colonial rule doubtless contains some sordid chapters, and some that we might well wish that we could rewrite. But those who read the story will find it lightened by much which we can have no cause to regret, and by some things indeed which have enriched the record of the better achievements of the human spirit.[25]

Others too were prepared to accept some criticism in relation to the distant past only to reject it for the present.

To take a few examples. William Crocker wrote in 1947: 'Imperialism in the ugly sense is, over the greater part of Africa, dead'. Harold Ingham, head of public relations in the Colonial Office wrote in a Confidential Print distributed throughout the Empire:

> The truth perhaps is that in so far as the evils of a capitalist system have been found to result in exploitation, etc., they have been at least partially abated, simply because it has not, for a very long time, been in our national character to tolerate exploitation. Such evils as remain as part of the marks of imperialism are the result, not of colonial policy, but of the outlook of individuals and groups of individuals.[26]

Even the partial concessions about economic exploitation in the distant past tended to be heavily qualified. Hailey attempted to limit the damage further by stating that exploitation had never been systematic: 'no one can pretend that the aim was always altruistic' but this 'does not prove the existence of a deliberate and continuous policy of acquisition'. Burns's classic *In Defence of Colonies* took the view that exploitation was merely one aspect of British imperialism: 'there was undoubtedly the desire for trade and the profits expected to accrue from that trade, but there were other motives also and the spread of Christianity was not the least of them'.[27] Such arguments had the effect of diminishing the negative side of the imperial record.

Many publicists argued that the critics of Empire failed to acknowledge that the situation in many parts of the world was far worse before colonialism than after. Margery Perham dismissed the view that 'African poverty and backwardness is due mainly to British exploitation' on the grounds that this 'is a poor continent'. This was also the argument of Rita Hinden of the Fabian Colonial Bureau: 'the fact is that, even before the entry of imperialist powers the colonial territories were poor and economically backward'. Creech-Jones assured his readers that it was not 'due to rapacious capitalism or modern exploiting "colonialism"' that colonies were poor: 'Much of what is wrong in under-developed societies comes because of the poverty of nature and the backwardness of people who have been insulated for centuries by ignorance and superstition.'[28] According to this scenario poverty predated colonialism. By posing poverty as an original sin forced on the colonies by nature, imperialist exploitation was explained away as a minor footnote in history.

History was also rewritten in an extraordinarily brazen manner in order to legitimise Empire. In Hailey's account most West Indian islands were uninhabited, just waiting for British settlement. Malaya was 'ceded by local Sultans' and three of the Malay states 'voluntarily applied for British protection'! According to Harlow the threat of pirates and brigands to Chinese traders caused Britain to assume control over Malaya. At other times the reverse argument could be used for the same purpose. Whereas Harlow implied that it was the defence of the Chinese that motivated the British occupation of Malaya, in 1948 Rees-Williams demanded propaganda to show 'that it was owing to the failure of the Malaya to control the Chinese in the States that the British were called in'.[29] The central message of all these histories of Empire was that there was no inherent expansionary dynamic within imperialism, and that the motives of British colonialism were more often honourable than not.

Finally there was a major campaign to expunge the word imperialism from the language, on the grounds that it falsely attributed immoral motives to Western foreign policy. The term almost invariably appeared with quote marks around it to warn off the reader. Alternatively the term was dismissed by a literary sleight of hand. Crocker's approach was typical. 'A beginning might well be made', he noted in passing, 'by banning the portmanteau bogey word imperialism'. Having asserted the irrelevance of the term as if it were common sense, Crocker swiftly moved on to other matters. The habit of dismissing the relevance of the term imperialism through an aside continues to this day.[30]

One of the most common methods for discrediting the charge of imperialism was by calling into question the motives of those who used the term. Defenders of Empire never tired of pointing out that, presumably unlike them, those who insisted upon attacking the West as imperialist were motivated either by ideology or by some other disreputable impulse. Perham typifies this approach in her 1944 statement to an American readership:

> The strongest attacks on imperialism from an economic point of view, inspired by Communist doctrine, seem to come from Negro intellectuals who have grievances of their own against white capitalism.[31]

Subversives and individuals with a chip on their shoulders were the ones likely to attack imperialism. It was a 'hate word' according to Koebner and Schmidt. They added that 'Lenin's theory of imperialism was suitable for propaganda among the half-educated whose power of criticism was not fully developed'.[32] In this way, innuendo and bitter invective against the integrity of those who used the term served as a substitute for a critique of the concept of imperialism. The sheer volume of material designed to belittle the term exposed the anxieties of the defenders of Empire.

Rewriting History

The rearguard action to discredit attacks upon imperialism and colonialism was not confined to those closely linked to the British Empire. Intellectuals from other Western societies such as France and the United States also took part in this project. Even those who were not directly involved in the study of imperial themes were drawn towards a similar perspective. The Cold War environment created a situation where the charge of imperialism was a weapon that the Soviet Union could use against its opponents. This was a factor that could not be ignored by Western intellectuals when the ideological battlelines were drawn. As Seymour Lipset, the ardent defender of American liberalism observed, 'in Asia and Africa the longterm presence of colonial rulers has identified conservative ideology and the more well-to-do classes with subservience to colonialism, while leftist ideologies, usually of a Marxist variety, have been identified with nationalism'.[33] No doubt this explains why Western liberals and conservatives were so keen to minimise the role of imperialism.

The tendency to rewrite history by minimising the destructive role of imperialism became such an obsession that examples of it could be found in the strangest of places. So for example, a liberal text directed against bias in history criticised post Second World War German school books for drawing attention to the economic aspects of the British Empire:

> Too much is said about the economic and military side of British impe-rialism, too little about the role of religion in the foundation of the early colonies. Similarly, the abolition of slavery in the British Empire in 1833 is sometimes attributed solely to economic motives, whereas every Englishman knows that pure philanthropy played a prominent part indeed.[34]

This whitewashing of imperialism, the good bits always outweighing the bad, is a consistent theme in Western literature. It is no less evident in American than in British contributions.[35]

A close inspection of the literature of the 1940s, 1950s and 1960s reveals that most of the conservative and liberal thinkers of the time actively participated in the retrospective defence of Western imperial expansion and colonialism. Many of the key figures active in defending the West during the Cold War were also committed to the rehabilitation of the imperial past. One reason, perhaps, why this tendency has not been widely discussed was the manner in which the arguments were conducted. Comments on imperialism were usually made through casual hints and throw-away remarks in texts that were often about other subjects. The anti-imperialist climate of the time must have made a more explicit defence of the Western imperial past more difficult to pursue.

To give a flavour of this literature. Hans Kohn, who was a bitter critic of German historicism and the whole tradition of nationalist histori-ography, could nonetheless write a celebration of the British Empire in the following terms:

> The liberal imperialism of the nineteenth century was not only controlled by the recognized plurality of empires and by the restrain-ing force of the acknowledged validity of universal ethical standards above class or race, but its inner logic led to its own withering away. The process of decolonization, of increasing concessions to the inde-pendence of colonial peoples, had begun on the part of Britain, the leader in liberty well before the outbreak of the First World War.[36]

Kohn's arguments very much reflected the outlook of the postwar totalitarian theorists. Hannah Arendt, who wrote the major work on totalitarianism in the postwar era devoted a significant section to a discussion of imperialism. She shows considerable sensitivity to the development of racist and authoritarian sentiments through British imperialism, and yet she draws back from following through the logic of her analysis. She writes how the 'conscience of the nation' in Britain, called the 'imperial factor', created an 'imperialism with the merits and remnants of justice it so eagerly tried to eliminate'. According to Arendt 'the natives were not only protected but in a way represented' by the British Parliament.[37] This statement is all the more astounding in that it follows a vivid depiction of the growth of imperialist racialism in the nineteenth century.

Other Cold War intellectuals shared Arendt's approach. Raymond Aron's lecture 'Imperialism and Colonialism' suggests that France acquired its African Empire by accident and that no economic causation was involved.[38] For Aron the very idea of a structured causal link between capitalism and imperialism was anathema. Aron declared: 'how can we accept the proposition that colonial conquest is the extreme form, the inevitable expression, of an expansion inherent in capitalist economies?'.[39]

'The chief ideological passion in the world today is anti-imperialism', wrote Daniel Bell, a leading American intellectual, as a prelude to rubbishing this 'common rhetorical cry for Arab feudal sheiks, African nationalist leaders, and Latin American military dictators, as well as for left-wing revolutionaries'.[40] Bell's line of argument was standard in the campaign to whitewash imperialism. The argument did not so much defend imperialism as attack the moral authority of anti-imperialists. By emphasising the cynical manipulation of anti-colonial sentiments by 'feudal sheiks' and 'military dictators' the legitimacy of anti-imperialism as such was put to question.

Specialist contributions which dealt with the subject directly were far more explicit in their praise of imperialism. Rupert Emerson, an American expert on colonial societies, never missed an opportunity to praise Western expansion abroad:

> A plausible case can, however, be made from the proposition that the future will look back upon the overseas imperialism of recent centuries, less in terms of its sins of oppression, exploitation, and discrimination, than as the instrument by which the spiritual, scientific, and material revolution which began in Western Europe with the Renaissance was spread to the rest of the world.[41]

Emerson was of course not mainly concerned about the future. His rewriting of history was directed towards dealing with the ideological problems of his time.

The Fatal Flaw

The project of whitewashing imperialism helped to limit the damage. But it could not positively contribute to the reconstruction of imperial legitimacy. The arguments used to defend Western colonialism were too defensive to tackle the problem of imperial legitimation. The very indirect and apologetic manner in which they were usually presented indicated a lack of real conviction. The concessions made to anti-colonial nationalism made it difficult to restate the imperial case in a forceful form. In any case the decline of the European empires made it much harder to uphold the culture that was associated with them.

The weakness of the arguments were also due to the fact that sections of the political elite ceased to believe in themselves. In London, officials were at a loss as to how to answer the charge that Britain exploited its colonies. Although Whitehall officials routinely placed quotation marks around their use of the word 'exploitation', suggesting their incomprehension that doubts could be cast about imperial benevolence, there was a strong sense of apprehension that they might lose the argument. Some privately conceded the essentials of the charge, while many others were prepared to accept its truth for the practices of the past if not for the present. The comments of the Ministry of Information on a proposed propaganda campaign in West Africa in 1944 displayed this ambivalence:

> The question of 'exploitation' requires very careful handling. There is no doubt in the past that the big firms have not put back into Nigeria even a small fraction of what they have taken out. It is a complicated matter, and possibly it would be better to stress the future rather than the past.[42]

If British publicists even partially accepted the criticisms of imperial exploitation, then their arguments in defence of empire were likely to be less than razor sharp and unconvincing. In effect they refused to contest the criticisms made about the activities of British firms in the past. But the refusal to contest the terrain of the past was unlikely to provide Britain with effective propaganda in the present.

At the intellectual level the problem was the absence of any wholehearted justification of imperialism. The articles and books published on the subject during the 1940s and 1950s expose a lack of confidence toward the Empire. Few were prepared to provide an outright defence of Britain's imperial mission. Attempts to celebrate imperialism, like T.E. Utley's 'The Imperialist Tradition', were very much the exception.[43] Instead of defending imperialism, British and American intellectuals sought to deny it had ever existed. Thus they abandoned that which had inspired their own political identity a few years earlier. Imperialism was simply written out of existence.

Most criticisms of the Marxist theory of imperialism were essentially attempts at denying the very existence of the phenomenon. This was a short-term expedient, which had the long-term effect of discrediting the traditional political culture of the West. In effect the Cold War intelligentsia, by denying the centrality of the imperial identity to Western society, were denying their own past. They did not question the charge that imperialism was something to be ashamed about; they merely denied all association with it.

The American Cold War ideologue Louis Feuer, was one of the first to recognise the fatal consequences of imperialism denial. He argued that, for the West, the denial of imperialism was as problematic as the anti-imperialist critique itself. He astutely reminded his readers:

> The ablest critics of the Hobson-Lenin thesis, while demolishing its economic arguments, nonetheless wish themselves to be regarded as basically among the opponents of imperialism. Such historical analysts as D.K. Fieldhouse thus regard imperialism as a 'delusion' and 'irrational'.[44]

Feuer recognised that the attempt to distance the West from imperialism was in the long run counterproductive. By denying imperialism the Western elite was denying itself. It was distancing itself from its past. And consequently it could not regain its moral authority, since it would be vulnerable to fundamental criticisms about what it stood for. Feuer's call for the moral rehabilitation of imperialism in the West was prescient. But the attempt to initiate that project would have to wait a few years, until the end of the Cold War.

Although the weakness of the pro-imperial arguments was seldom explicitly acknowledged by their proponents, implicitly there was a recognition that they had a problem. To compensate for the weakness of their arguments they tended not so much to defend imperialism as to rubbish anti-colonial movements. Official propagandists in London seemed more comfortable projecting negative propaganda against their opponents than trying to win the case for Empire. It seemed easier to be negative about colonial nationalism than to be positive about British achievements. Instead of being able to win moral authority on their own accounts, Western publicists directed their fire at the low morality of others. The virulent invective directed at the Third World, alluded to in previous chapters, was at least in part motivated by this consideration.

Anti Third World Ideology

Positive arguments in defence of the Empire in the end proved less convincing than propaganda aimed at discrediting anti-colonial movements. From the point of view of British publicists, the virtue of negative arguments was that they shifted the focus of attention away from the record of Empire and on to the morals of its opponents. By questioning the integrity, motives and behaviour of individuals and movements in the Third World, the moral superiority of Britain could be upheld, and attention diverted away from the awkward questions about colonial exploitation and conquest. Although this approach was unlikely to convince people in the colonies, it could be surprisingly effective with a British and Western audience.

Advocates of Empire usually argued that, whatever the problem with a particular colony or imperial policy, those who opposed it were far worse. The former Governor of the Gold Coast, Sir Alan Burns's *In Defence of Colonies* provides a paradigm for this type of argument. At times Burns almost abandons a positive defence of Empire. Instead he opts for the approach of demonstrating how the alternative to Empire is so much worse. He explains away the difficulty of ending racial discrimination in the Empire by pointing to the failure of India to abolish caste untouchability. In the same manner those who criticise imperial coercion are dismissed with the following words:

> Those whose indignation is aroused when British aircraft bomb Mau Mau murderers, or raiders in the Aden protectorate, do not seem to be disturbed when Pakistani aircraft bomb a concentration of Afridi tribesmen killing 34 and wounding 16.

Pakistani atrocities lighten the burden of British responsibility for its cavalier use of force in the colonies. In the same way the deployment of draconian emergency powers by Britain is excused by pointing to the use of such restrictions in India, Cuba or 'generally by the Governments of the Arab States'. Finally poverty in British colonies is 'placed in perspective' by arguing that life is far worse in Guatemala and Haiti. The reader is also informed that the 'indigenous Amerindian population … is much less "free" than the people of a British colony'.[45]

The attempt to vindicate Empire through pointing at the real or alleged failing of others was actively pursued by Whitehall. The Foreign Office demanded comparative data to show that independent Third World countries like Liberia or Haiti were worse off than British colonies.[46] It is worth noting that the official 'comparative' approach was quickly picked up by pro-Empire scholars. Thus Rupert Emerson wrote that a 'factor serving to lessen the ill repute of colonialism is the comparison frequently drawn between countries that have had an intensive experience of Western colonial rule, and other underdeveloped areas that have had none or only a brief touch of it'.[47]

American writers were also quick to point at alleged failings of others so as to justify the actions of Washington. 'For all the domestic ills or foreign "crimes" of the United States, its record as a civilized society commands respect – especially compared to the savageries of the Soviet Union or Germany or the newer states of Rwanda, Burundi and Uganda – and we need not be apologetic on that score', wrote Daniel Bell.[48]

The negative comparisons with the Third World were complemented by studies which suggested that it was the internal weakness of these societies rather than colonialism which constituted the real problem. The substance of the argument was that the Third World was congenitally incapable of looking after its own affairs. Chaos, decay and corruption were the characteristics associated with independent postcolonial states. Typically, the colonial era was presented as something of a golden age. Problems were always portrayed as the fault of Third World societies. The evidence that imperialism had left behind a legacy of difficulties was invariably rejected.

An article on 'Britain's Imperial Legacy' published in the 1950s in the influential American journal *Foreign Affairs*, expressed the classic Anglo-American wisdom on the subject:

Should the British be blamed for the persistence and sometimes the aggravation of these internal divisions after independence? Many Asian and African nationalists have talked of a sinister policy of 'divide and rule' whereby the British stirred up local hostilities in order to delay the transfer of power. But since self-government has, in virtually all cases, been granted, the accusation of conspiracy can hardly be sustained. The critics forget two factors – the degree to which the institutions introduced by contact with Britain require a certain measure of communal unity and the time it takes to overcome religious, linguistic and racial diversity by broader loyalties.[49]

This was the standard response against the argument that the problems of the Third World were a legacy of imperialism. Gradually, decade by decade the arguments against the Third World became stronger and more extravagant.

By the mid 1970s, periodicals like *Foreign Affairs* and even more liberal journals were depicting the Third World as a frightening threat to global peace. It was now the West that was the victim and the Third World guerrilla, the aggressor. An article in *Foreign Affairs* in July 1975 is typical of the more aggressive style of anti Third World propaganda:

> The generations that have come to maturity in Europe and America since the end of the Second World War have asked only to bask in the sunshine of a summertime world; but they have been forced instead to live in the fearful shadow of other people's deadly quarrels. Gangs of politically motivated gunmen have disrupted everyday life intruding and forcing their parochial feuds upon the unwilling attention of everybody else.[50]

The idyllic image of a peaceful West is placed in sharp contrast to the evil that emanates from the Third World. Certainly by the 1980s, the characteristics most often associated with Third World movements are brutality, corruption, senseless violence and above all *terror*.

The deployment of negative arguments in defence of Empire has continued throughout the postwar era. For much of this period the West has abandoned a positive promotion of itself, and instead inflated the blemishes of Third World societies. Thus the many upheavals and disasters in Third World countries are continually highlighted in order to rehabilitate the empires by suggesting that things are now far worse than during the colonial experience. Elton is scathing of 'liberal myths' about the British Empire. He states that post-colonial states in the 1960s 'killed far more people in previously imperial territories than 200 years of building these empires ever destroyed'. Lord Beloff argued along similar lines that 'famine, civil and tribal war and genocide are the direct result of what we might style the catastrophe of decolonization'.[51]

A Call for Revenge

Negative arguments, which were gradually transformed into a system of ideas – anti Third World ideology – became the main intellectual response to the anti-colonial challenge during the 1940s and 1950s. Nationalist leaders like Mossadeqh, Peron, Nasser, Nkrumah or Sukarno were systematically portrayed as insane, megalomaniacal, power-hungry, irrational and fanatical. The movements they personified were represented in the same unflattering terms. The tendency to criminalise and morally condemn Third World nationalism provided a ready-made idiom through which the challenge to the West could be explained.

These arguments developed over many decades. During the 1940s and 1950s the Cold War obliged many Western officials to acknowledge the new anti-colonial climate. Later, in the 1950s and 1960s, they had to go a step further and to seek an accommodation with anti-colonial movements. But this public attempt to come to terms with Third World nationalism existed alongside the basic Western suspicions about 'them'. So while Western diplomats courted the leaders of the newly independent states, others, usually in the popular media, reminded people of the threats posed by 'those' societies.

Those in the know could reconcile pragmatic diplomatic concerns with their discreet assumption of moral superiority. Every setback or problem in the Third World could be interpreted as confirmation of what the West privately knew to be true. Events like the Congo crisis of 1960 would serve as reminders of eternal truths about the *real* character of the African. As Rupert Emerson remarked, 'for many Americans, the entire Congo experience and the murder of hostages in particular had a drastic effect in rearousing the image of Africans as a savage and primitive people'.[52] In other words, when something went wrong there was a popular Western explanation at hand which would view events in Africa from the vantage point of superiority. Emerson failed to add that the media made sure that it was the sensationalist accounts of brutal treatment of whites which focused the imagination of the American public.

The success of anti Third World ideas in influencing Western societies did not automatically mean that the crisis of imperialist legitimacy was resolved. The dramatic events of the 1960s revealed that the Western political elites still faced fundamental difficulties in coming to terms with the legacy of imperialism. This was a time when the Third World occupied the moral highground and the West was in disarray. The experience of Algeria for France and Vietnam for the United States underlined the dimensions of the problem. America's 'Vietnam Syndrome', the loss of a sense of mission and self-belief which followed defeat in south-east Asia, symbolised the difficulties faced by all imperialist powers. The attraction of Che Guevara and notions of

Third Worldism for many Western middle-class youth suggested that the ideological battle was far from won. For influential leaders in the West, the 1960s were a traumatic experience. For a while it even appeared that the Third World cause could occupy the moral highground indefinitely.

Partly in reaction to the 1960s, the 1970s were marked by the intensification of anti Third World rhetoric. The right in particular became more and more aggressive, and attacks on Third World societies became more explicit. Increasingly, the emphasis was placed not just on condemning these societies but also on warning of the danger they represented. It is in this period that the myth of the international terrorist emerges with full force.

In the 1970s the anti Third World pronouncements also become more bitter. Thus we find the British Field Marshal, Sir Gerald Templar, explaining away the end of Empire as the fault of the 'underground activities of Marxism' always 'encouraged by the inborn hatred of anything which could be termed colonialism'. The Thatcherite historian Hugh Thomas warned:

> He who condemns the evils of colonialism must not be allowed to forget that the almost daily ritual murder, or the golden stools coated with blood and swarming with flies, which characterised Ashanti in the 1860s. 'Imperialism' drew the neglected parts of the world into the general sweep of human history.[53]

A new literature was emerging. In France the 'new philosophers' poured scorn on Islam and repressive Third World governments. In America and Britain, led by the new right, it became fashionable to condemn the moral claims of Third World societies.

By the 1980s much of the literature on the Third World amounted to a call for retaliation, for revenge of past wrongs. The loss of moral authority could now be avenged. The suggestion seemed to be that the credibility of the West depended on discrediting the societies of the Third World. The underlying conviction was that through criminalising the Third World the West could morally rehabilitate itself. This required going on to the offensive. Whether the West is truly capable of going on the offensive remains to be seen. This, the revenge of the West, is the subject of the final chapter.

6   The Moral Rehabilitation of Imperialism

Our aim so far has not been to celebrate the virtues of Third World nationalism but to explore how and why this phenomenon has been manipulated and demonised by the West. The limitations of the nationalist programme itself should be clear to all. However, the era of anti-colonial nationalism coincided with some important positive developments. These were the growth of egalitarian consciousness – the questioning of the right of one nation to dominate another. Finally this period saw the discrediting of imperialism in all of its aspects. For the first time there was the recognition that the social, economic and political problems of the Third World, from repression to hunger, were integrally connected to Western domination. Imperialism was held responsible for the crises in these societies. Today, even this insight is being blurred. The ever-strengthening consensus of our times is that the problems of the Third World stem from its own moral or cultural limitations, and that one way or another the solution lies in the hands of the Western powers. Worse still, the Third World is being held responsible for many of the problems facing Western societies.

There has been a dramatic shift in the discussion around the theme of Third World nationalism and imperialism. The anti-colonial moment has been overtaken by an era in which imperialism is no longer so defensive. Indeed today it is *not colonialism but decolonisation* that is likely to be treated as problematic. It is not colonialism but the abuse of independence that is held responsible for the ills which afflict African and Asian societies. According to the British establishment historian G.R. Elton, the dissolution of the colonial empires was a colossal error. Pointing to the 'millions of dead in the wake of European withdrawal', Elton has only scorn for decolonisation. At the launch of his book *Churchill: The End of Glory*, historian John Charmley also had no inhibitions about denouncing decolonisations as evil:

> The British Empire vanishing has had a very deleterious effect on the third world. Look at Uganda under the British and look at it now. And you didn't get famines quite as frequently in Africa then as you do now.[1]

Such bold affirmation of imperialism, while not yet commonplace, is no longer exceptional. Douglas Hurd, the British Secretary of State for Foreign Affairs, noted with a sigh of relief that 'we are slowly puting behind us a period of history when the West was unable to express a legitimate interest in the developing world without being accused of "neo-colonialism".'[2] This positive promotion of the record of imperialism is part of a discourse which is very different to the traditional anti Third World ideology discussed previously.

In Chapter 5 we looked at how, throughout the postwar era, Western ideologists had been forced largely to abandon the positive promotion of imperialism and to concentrate instead on promoting negative images of its opponents. Since the 1980s, however, there has been a significant sea-change in the climate of discussion. Instead of merely discrediting Third World societies there is now a new attempt *positively* to celebrate the record of the West – and in the process, morally to rehabilitate imperialism.

Since the late 1980s the defensive rhetoric of the West has become far less pronounced. At the same time the anti Third World themes of Western political culture have become increasingly vitriolic. Now the anti-colonial standpoint is on the retreat. The aftermath of the 1991 Gulf War against Iraq was marked by a tendency expressly to celebrate imperial conquest in Britain and the United States. For the first time in half a century, the term imperialism was openly used in a positive sense. Influential publications like the *Wall Street Journal* in the United States or *The Times* in Britain now regularly express this sentiment. The mood of turning the clock back to the grand days of Empire was expressed by the *Wall Street Journal* when it suggested that the USA had been wrong to stop Britain and France from invading Colonel Nasser's Egypt during the Suez crisis of 1956: 'Perhaps the biggest strategic mistake in the postwar era', it noted, was 'shrinking from the British and French use of force against Nasser'.[3] One academic, well known in the field of international relations, boasted that 'the West is now more secure and confident in the superiority of its values than it has been at any time since the end of the Second World War'.[4]

The emergence of a new, more overt Western imperial rhetoric is the product of three separate but mutually reinforcing causes. These are, first, the failure of what has been called Third Worldism. Second, the emergence of a conservative intellectual climate, which is the product of the decline of various other social experiments. And third, the end of the Cold War, which has removed one of the major restraints on Western intervention in Third World societies.

Western ideologues have drawn tremendous satisfaction from the failures of various Third World revolutions and from the disintegration of post-colonial societies. This reaction has been evident since the 1960s, by which time every coup in Africa and Asia was presented as confirmation of the thesis that independence had been premature. The economic, political, and military crises which afflict post-colonial societies serve as a sort of retrospective justification for imperialism. Feuer's reflections on conflict in contemporary Africa take the form of a reprimand of anti-imperialists:

> The abrogation of imperialism brought a resurgence of tribal massacres in independent African states. Untrammelled aggression exceeded the bounds imaginable by the most sceptical of Western imperialists.[5]

Civil wars, ethnic conflicts, economic collapse and famines are all used to demolish the moral credibility of different regimes in Africa and Asia. That the various anti-imperialist regimes have failed to sustain popular support has helped the campaign to vindicate colonialism retrospectively. One international relations expert noted that 'the euphoria of independence has faded' and with a hint of triumphalism added that the 'reality of continued inferiority has reasserted itself'.[6] The responsibility of imperialism for creating conditions in which independence was little more than a fiction is passed over in silence.

The campaign against the moral authority of Third World societies thrived in the conservative intellectual climate of the 1980s. The failure of various radical and anti-capitalist experiments stimulated an inhospitable climate for critical ideas. This period brought the disillusionment with anti-imperialist politics among liberal and radical intellectuals in the West. Consequently, by the time of the war against Iraq, there was virtually no intellectual critique of the West's right to intervene militarily in the Third World.

The collapse of the Soviet Union and the termination of the Cold War was the most decisive factor in changing the terms of the relationship between the West and the Third World. As long as the Soviet bloc was in existence the West was prevented from reasserting its hegemony over the Third World in an open form. Even as the campaign to demonise Third World regimes got into full swing in the 1970s, Western diplomats with one eye on the Soviets were forced to accommodate and even court the leaders of African and Asian societies. But with the decline and demise of the Soviet Union, Western governments are under no pressure to carry on this charade.

'The collapse of Russian power has altered everything', exclaimed John Casey, the right-wing Cambridge academic:

> The deference liberals in the West have shown towards the various nationalisms of the Third World could be understood, not as the application of highminded principle but as part of the Western, and especially American strategy of wooing those who might otherwise succumb to communists blandishments.
>
> But, with the collapse of Soviet communism, the old colonial powers, along with America, can now do what they like. There is no longer any need to take seriously things like Arab nationalism, or the allegedly unjust divisions imposed on the Arab world by the colonial powers.[7]

Casey's observation that the Western powers 'can now do what they like' captures the remarkable turnaround in the balance of international power. He concludes on a note of smugness, 'Those of us who have never disavowed the imperialist past nor sought to cloak national interest with moral sanctimoniousness will not be troubled by this'. Some intellectuals on the right celebrated the end of the Cold War even more for its consequences in the Third World than for the defeat of the Soviet Union.[8] For some, the possibility of openly condemning Third World nationalism in all of its aspects was an exhilarating prospect. 'Bring Back Lord Kitchener?' was the title of a contribution in the *Wall Street Journal*, which sought to reaffirm America's imperial mission to 'avoid a world constantly diminished, and even threatened, by future Bosnias, Somalias, Haitis and Iraqis'.[9]

The Intellectual Annihilation of Third World Nationalism

The overt imperial triumphalism of the *Wall Street Journal* and of American and British right-wing writers expresses sentiments which, in a more inhibited form, exist throughout these societies today. The commentary of the mainstream on these matters is still guarded and hesitant. But the right's triumphalism is consistent with the prevailing intellectual currents. The whole anti-colonial experience now tends to be treated with derision, and Third World nationalism is dismissed as an act of bad faith. This climate of scorn has important consequences in undermining the legitimacy of anti-imperialism. The tendency to devalue the Third World nationalist culture implicitly calls into question the whole anti-imperialist project. In the present climate every negative experience in the Third World is depicted as further proof of the unworthy character of the challenge to imperialism.

Often the old-fashioned prejudices against anti-colonial nationalism are recycled in the currently fashionable language of postmodernism. It is often suggested that in the postmodern world the old traditional identities have exposed the pretensions of modernism and nationalism. According to these explanations modernism is but a momentary illusion. One writer points to a 'confusing clash between pre-modern traditionalism, liberal democracy and the intensification of media politics in highly unpredictable and novel conjunctures from Eastern Europe to the Middle East'.[10] The thrust of the argument is always to underline the illusory character of nationalist aspirations, or at least to emphasise the ineffectiveness of Third World nationalism in overcoming the older traditions.

The upsurge of communal and ethnic tensions throughout the world is now translated into the proposition that nationalism was but a hallucination. Writers are prepared to talk of 'tribal nationalism' or 'ethnic nationalism' or some other parochial form of this phenomenon, but not of nationalism as such. For example, according to an editorial in *US News and World Report*, nationalism in the Third World has proven to be a fraud:

> In the Third World, there had been grand ideas of new states and social contracts among the communities, post-colonial dreams of what men and women could do on their own. There were exalted notions of Indian nationalism, Pan-Arabism and the like. Ethnicity hid, draped in the colors of modern nationalism, hoping to keep the ancestors – and the troubles – at bay. But the delusions would not last. What was India? The India of its secular founders –or the "Hindu Raj" of the militant fundamentalists? What exactly did the compact communities of Iraq – the Kurds, the Sunnis and the Shia – have in common? The masks have fallen, the tribes have stepped to the fore.[11]

According to this interpretation, nationalism was an artificial construction that could not overcome the legacy of the past. As a consequence, the argument goes, the late twentieth century is characterised by the 'resurgence of ethnic nationalism'.[12]

According to the new wisdom, the lack of substance to Third World nationalism is demonstrated by the survival of traditional or primordial sentiments. Daniel Yankelovich, the President of the American Public Agenda Foundation, observed that the end of the Cold War has 'unleashed the passions of ethnic tribalism all over the world'.[13] Yankelovich, in line with current thinking, takes it for granted that these 'age-old' passions have survived from an earlier time. The implication is that the period of nationalist agitation and of decolonisation did not alter the unyielding reality of 'ethnic tribalism'. According to some versions of the argument, the clock has been turned back to the realities of the nineteenth century. The *Washington Post* situates America's latest adventure in Somalia from this perspective:

> This is a disorienting trip back to a square one that political history was supposed to have left behind, moving in a straight line from empire, wars of national liberation, decolonization and on to independence. But the nightly footage of the shattered streets of Mogadishu shows that history has a reverse gear too.[14]

This conservative analysis is based on the simplistic proposition that African and Asian societies remain steeped in the past. The post-colonial era could neither come to terms with nor overcome these primordial forces, and therefore became irrelevant. Anti-colonialism, the struggle for independence and the post-colonial experience are thus transformed into a minor depressing footnote alongside the great events of history.

The conservative view fatalistically accepts a kind of original sin thesis, whereby tribal conflict *is* the human condition – at least in Africa. 'An ancient plague, whose outbreaks are often bloody episodes like the one in Liberia, continues to afflict the people of sub-Saharan Africa', warns a major feature in *Newsweek*.[15] Against a hardy old 'ancient plague', there is no medicine.

Postmodern theories never consider the obvious questions. Why should ethnic consciousness be ancient or any more natural than anti-colonial nationalism? Why should ethnic ties, as Anthony Smith suggests, be more durable and binding than other ones?[16] It is highly unlikely that so-called primordial passions have survived intact, or that somehow they have existed above history, waiting to make a comeback. It is far more fruitful to view the conflicts that have erupted throughout the world not as the revenge of the past, but as the products of a contemporary crisis of political legitimacy. It is not some dynamic ancient identity that drives the participants in numerous civil wars, but the failure of the national system to provide an effective unitary focus for their loyalty. In other words, the ethnic tribes of the contemporary Western imagination do not precede anti-colonial nationalism; they are a reaction to it.

The promotion of parochial identities today represents a return to the theories of British imperialist publicists of the early part of this century. The theory of indirect rule, associated with Lord Lugard, suggested that the authentic African was the 'man of tradition' rather than the detribalised native. This focus on parochial-traditional identity also conveniently questioned the legitimacy of the nationalist. The nationalist was not a genuine African. In the same vein, the proposition that traditional identities have returned annuls the legitimacy of anti-colonial nationalism.

An article 'Africa and the New World Dis-order' by Francis Deng, published by the Brookings Institute, is paradigmatic of the contemporary anti-nationalist contributions. Unlike many other contributions, this is a relatively liberal presentation of the argument. Deng seems genuinely concerned about the plight of Africa and he avoids the bitter rhetoric of some of his colleagues. Nevertheless, his approach is actually reminiscent of the criticism that paternalistic imperialists used to make of colonial interference in the life of indigenous people. For example, he criticises colonialism for undermining the old indigenous, legitimate authorities. Deng takes to task colonialism for divesting the 'local communities and ethnic groups of much of their indigenous autonomy'. However, for reason's which are not explained, these communities have somehow survived the colonial experience intact. Deng writes:

> Old identities, undermined and rendered dormant by the structures and values of the nation-state system, are reemerging and redefining the standards of participation, distribution and legitimacy.

By definition the reassertion of these old identities represents the negation of anti-colonial nationalism. For Deng, they are the authentic manifestation of African culture, whereas nationalism is an artificial implant. Deng's solution is to rid Africa of the alien scourge of nationalism. The author follows through the logic of his argument, concluding with a call for a 'new Berlin Conference' to rework the borders of Africa.[17]

Deng's analysis is part of the consensus against Third World nationalism that embraces almost the entire political spectrum in the West. Many former critics of imperialism have become demoralised by the failure of once-fashionable Third World regimes. Many who uncritically celebrated a succession of nationalist leaders in the past now uncritically accept that these same nationalists are to blame for everything. The reaction against anti-colonial nationalism is particularly dramatic among those who not so long ago worshipped at its altar. The most systematic exposition of this reaction is contained in Basil Davidson's

The Black Man's Burden: Africa and the Curse of the Nation-State. Davidson's book has been highly acclaimed both in the media and by academic specialists. By considering the main thesis of *The Black Man's Burden* it is possible to gain some important insights into the current anti-nationalist fashion.

Davidson's thesis is devastatingly simple. He argues that African nationalists have in effect accepted an alien system of values which directly contradicts their own cultures. Nationalism is presented as the alienation of the African intellectual. In a language reminiscent of the imperial discourse around the theme of the spiritual vacuum of the detribalised African, Davidson argues that the alienation caused by nationalism is the cause of the violence of post-colonial Africa. To the pathological violence of the alienated nationalist Davidson counterposes a roman-ticised representation of tribal society in which violence was kept in check by an accepted moral code.[18]

Davidson is clearly enchanted by the tribal and the traditional. This concern has been praised by many academics because it provides a positive presentation of Africa's past. However, attempts to reclaim the past are always problematic. In this case the attempt to derive a viable political culture from the pre-colonial era requires more than a little myth-making. For example, Davidson attempts to elaborate a democratic political culture in pre-colonial Africa. As part of the evidence supporting this thesis, he presents the African's 'inbuilt distrust of executive power'.[19] However, the attempt to impose historically specific concepts of democracy on to societies of another age, with an entirely different political make-up, requires a level of generalisation that verges on the banal. To equate modes of consultation practised in Africa 200 years ago with those of today is to compare like with unlike. In any case, why should centuries-old tradition have any relevance for Africa today?

Actually, in a roundabout way, Davidson forcefully echoes the mistrust of the colonial administrator towards the nationalist politician. His sympathy is clearly with the traditional authority:

> When the Gold Coast Colony and Protectorate eventually became independent Ghana in 1957, the celebrations were both vivid and popular. But the king of Asante was not present at them. He refused to attend the great festivities of Independence Day. For him, as for others of his kind, this independence could only be a perverse denial of the old independence, and the new nationalism no more than usurpers of the legacy of Africa's own development.[20]

From this perspective, moral authority resides with the traditional leader. And national independence is presented as regression. The most eloquent colonial official could not have annihilated African nationalism's claim to legitimacy more thoroughly than Davidson.[21]

The celebration of ethnic identity is based on a profoundly conservative view of the world. It suggests, to be effective, that all actions must be based upon tradition. Any form of intervention in society which is inconsistent with the principles of past cultures is bound to fail. This limits the latitude for human experimentation and action. The question of what happens if past tradition proves inconsistent with human emancipation is not even posed. The past is presented as unproblematic, and what needs to be done is to make human action consistent with that tradition. The proposition that the parochial institutions of the past disintegrated precisely because they could not cope with the new circumstances of the modern world is not even entertained. Instead, without any serious substantiation, experts assert that democracy today depends on being in tune with Africa's pre-colonial culture.[22]

The main political legacy of celebrating traditional culture is to transform Third World nationalism into an all-purpose monster responsible for every disaster that has afflicted post-colonial societies. By comparison, colonialism and imperialism escape relatively unscathed. The consensus is that the cause of the many catastrophes is to be found not in the colonial but in the nationalist era. A major blow has been struck in the battle to rehabilitate imperialism.

Regardless of the intentions of proponents of the anti-nationalist thesis, its consequence is to flatter the self-image of the West through the rewriting of history. The Third World challenge – such as the Algerian, Chinese, Cuban or Vietnamese revolutions – represented a major blow both to the power and the confidence of imperialism. Whatever the subsequent trajectories of the societies concerned, at the time these events were seen as some of the most decisive events of the epoch. The denigration of this anti-imperialist experience violates history as it was lived. Aijaz Ahmad is to the point when he reminds the reader, 'That anti-colonial nationalism was a tremendous historical force until about the mid 1970s is a fact. That this force declined sharply in succeeding years is also a fact.'[23] The problem is that the starting point of anti-colonial nationalism, the liberationary impulse of the oppressed, has now been confused with its final outcome – the collapse of post-colonial nations. This confusion is the intellectual precondition for the rehabilitation of imperialism.

Redrawing Maps

Deng's call for a new Berlin Conference is not as eccentric as it may appear. The Berlin Conference which presided over the partitioning of Africa during the nineteenth century coincided with an outburst of imperialist rivalry and colonial conquest. It can be argued that aspects of this pattern are also evident in our own era.

Until recently, the idea of open conflict among the imperialist powers in the Third World would have been unthinkable. The Cold War artificially suspended or at least limited the rivalry between different Western powers. In any case the dominant position of the United States helped establish a global order with a clearly defined balance of power. Consequently, this was a period of unprecedented co-operation between Western powers. The North Atlantic Treaty Organisation symbolised this co-operation and suggested that diplomatic conflict between Western powers would be restricted to secondary issues. Co-operation and clearly defined rules characterised the period 1945–89.

The end of the Cold War at once spelled the demise of the old world order. With the disintegration of the Soviet Union, the cement of anti-communism could no longer bind together the Western powers. NATO had lost its purpose and there was no substitute for Cold War ideology to provide coherence to the Western alliance. The collapse of one superpower in the East coincided with the weakening of the other in the West. The United States, the main guarantor of the postwar world order, had become weaker as an economic power. The new ascendancy of Germany and Japan coincided with America's decline, thus helping to establish a multipolar international system. The end of the Cold War unfroze international relations and brought these underlying changes to the surface. The consequence was dramatic. The rules which governed the global system in the past have become irrelevant. The basis for the international co-operation that characterised the period 1945–89 no longer exists.

With the restraints imposed by the Cold War gone, the resurgence of a more open imperialist political culture is clear. The most obvious example of this development is the changing relationship of the West to the Third World. In the Western worldview the Third World has replaced the Soviet Union as the premier threat to stability. Anti Third world ideology may be a poor cousin to anti-Soviet rhetoric, but it still provides the main motive for international action. The shift towards confronting the Third World is also important for rebuilding a viable imperialist culture. The criminalisation of Third World regimes is crucial for the realisation of this project.

The main focus of this book has been on the contest for moral, intellectual and ideological legitimacy between the West and anti-colonial nationalists. This emphasis is justified, not on the grounds that it is necessarily the most important issue, but because overcoming the problem of imperial legitimacy is the *precondition* for the development of a coherent imperialist culture. There is a direct line linking the moral rehabilitation of imperialism to the fashion for Western intervention and the redrawing of borders in the Third World.

The practical consequence of the demonisation of Third World nationalism is the *redefinition of national sovereignty*. To all intents and purposes there are today two types of nation: the ones that have the legitimate right to interfere in the life of others, and the ones that have no intrinsic moral authority to run their own affairs. The campaign which calls into question the legitimacy and moral integrity of Third World societies also implicitly calls into question their right to exist. Such societies directly invite intervention. The absence of any serious criticism of Western intervention in Panama, Iraq, Somalia or Bosnia suggests that new conventions towards the management of international affairs have already been accepted.

There is now a considerable literature which argues the case for intervention. 'Acts of intervention may sometimes stem from honourable motives and sound judgement rather than in every case, from moral turpitude, disdain for the rule of law and indifference to world order', writes Inis Claude, adding that 'if the Panama intervention had useful results, it may be that what requires changing is not American foreign policy but the principle of non-intervention'. The rejection of the principle of non-intervention represents a justification of colonialism – so long as it is motivated by moral concerns. The case for colonialism is sustained through the vehement renunciation of assumptions of equality in international affairs. Claude argues that the principle of equality is 'obviously unrealistic' since the 'multistate system is marked by enormous disparities'.[24]

The moral case for Western intervention is seldom questioned today – the main focus of controversy is whether such interventions are practicable. According to William Pfaff, the well-known American commentator, 'any program of international intervention to keep order and check aggression would, in practice, seem to mean a mobilization of the Permanent members of the Security Council against conflict and unrest largely of Middle Eastern, Asian, African or Latin American origin'.[25] This unquestioned right of the great powers to intervene leads to a fundamental revision of the relationship between nation-states. There is a growing tendency to roll the film backwards from the era of independence to the age of colonial subjugation. It is as if some want to go full circle, back to the days before the acceptance of the right of nations to self-determination at the 1919 Paris Peace Conference.

The right to self-determination is under implicit, and sometimes explicit, attack. For example, James Mayall has argued that the acts of Third World tyrants have made this right redundant:

> Ostensibly, the most consistent public support for the idea of liberal international society came from the Third World. A large group of non-aligned, mostly ex-colonial, states asserted the continuing relevance of the principle of non-interference in the domestic affairs of other states. Since many of their governments were despotic tyrannies, their public commitment to the liberal vision failed to impress any but the most gullible of their Western supporters.[26]

A similar point is stressed by Jeffrey Herbst, who has argued that the norm of sovereignty was 'successfully used as a cover to repress those who challenged the existing nation-states' by African countries. Others have argued the case for ignoring national sovereignty as a barrier to Western intervention, on the grounds that 'every chaotic or anarchical situation has raised a call for some kind of order'. According to the French international relations specialist Pierre Hassner, the argument for ignoring national sovereignty has been already won: 'the legitimacy of international military intervention is no longer denied, as it once was, because it challenges state sovereignty or the principle of non-interference in internal affairs'.[27]

Hassner is absolutely right. Military intervention is now seen as an acceptable method for regulating relations between and within states. This practice is not yet justified explicitly; the United Nations charter, for example, still formally upholds the illegality of such interventions. A public attempt to rewrite international law in favour of intervention would risk raising embarrassing questions about what right the United States has to bomb buildings in Mogadishu, or about who gave Britain the authority to decide whether an election is fair in Nicaragua or Kenya. However, the lack of substantive criticism of Western adventures today means that the arguments in favour of intervention have been all but won. *De facto* if not *de jure*, the Western right to intervene in the affairs of other states now takes precedence over national sovereignty.

Saving the Third World from Itself

The widespread acceptance in the West of military intervention in other parts of the world is testimony to the effectiveness with which Third World nationalism has been discredited. The discrediting of anti-colonial movements has at the same time underwritten the West's claim to the moral high ground. Today, military intervention acquires its legitimacy through the manipulation of such moral claims. Intervention is not justified on militaristic grounds, as a glorious imperial mission. It is rationalised on the plane of morality, as a humanitarian act. The ostensible intention of Western intervention today is to save the Third World from itself.

Western diplomacy has routinely used political and economic instruments to interfere in the Third World, for example by confronting governments with an ultimatum to comply with a particular demand or face trade and credit sanctions. Since the late 1980s this kind of intervention has been used in pursuit of more far-reaching objectives. The need to protect ordinary people from local tyrants is now used as a pretext to dictate terms to Third World regimes. Robert Jackson remarked:

> Now that the Cold War is over and the Soviet Union is gone, Western governments and the international organizations they control are freer to place conduct requirements on sub-Saharan rulers. This could substantially reduce the freedom and influence of authoritarian regimes, more vulnerable and insecure today than they have been since independence.[28]

In this instance the case for intervention is justified on the grounds of assisting the restoration of democracy; the role of Western foreign policy in creating and sustaining the dictatorships concerned is quietly passed over. Others demand intervention to prevent chaos and save ordinary people from the terrible predicament in which their leaders have placed them. Robert Rotberg, an American specialist in African politics warned that 'Somalia cannot soon be left to itself' and observed that 'we should have ended the clan warfare earlier'.[29]

For Rotberg and Jackson, military intervention is a form of moral imperative. It is presented as a humanitarian gesture necessary to prevent famine, genocide or brutal aggression. In some cases even governmental incompetence constitutes a case for the new colonialism. A commentary on the ravages of a cyclone in Bangladesh in 1991 observed:

If the government of Bangladesh is too muddled and inept, as well as too poor, to build such shelters, then some foreign agency should intervene and build them directly. This is called neo-colonialism ... But in this case it seems hard to see why anyone should complain.[30]

The humanitarian focus is never absent. In Panama, the Americans invaded and destroyed the capital city in order to save the people from a drug-dealing tyrannical President. In Iraq, the salvation of suffering Kurds was portrayed as a key motif of the West's punitive military invasion. The invasion of Somalia was carefully labelled *Operation Restore Hope*. According to former US President George Bush, the objective of this adventure was no less than to do 'God's work' and 'save thousands of innocents'.

The Gulf War marked a turning point in the moral rehabilitation of imperialism. Outside of the Islamic world, no one seriously questioned the Western representation of events. Normally, an engagement which led to 147 Western casualties as against an estimated 100,000–200,000 Iraqi dead would have raised some serious questions. But this time the bombastic propaganda about the threat that Iraq posed was simply accepted. Indeed in the aftermath of this massacre Western liberal opinion demanded further military intervention in order to save the Kurds. The British liberal daily, the *Guardian* consistently expressed this standpoint. One of its feature writers pointed out:

US power, supported by European influence, and with the acquiescence of the Soviet Union, is the commanding fact in the Middle East today. We may squirm at the neo-colonial aspects of the use of such power, but that it ought to be used is undeniable.[31]

Liberals and leftists throughout the West put their squirming to one side and expressed similar sentiments.

It would be easy to argue that the arguments in favour of Western intervention are based on lies and media manipulation. For example anyone who cared to look could have found out that the wild stories about Iraqi nuclear capabilities were not just exaggerated but patently untrue. But it would be inappropriate to see these trends to mobilise Western intervention behind humanitarian banners in purely conspiratorial terms. Hobson's classic *Imperialism: A Study* offers useful insights into the role of the humanitarian impulse behind Western intervention.

As Hobson knew, nineteenth-century British colonialism was often justified through humanitarian sentiments. Expansion into Africa was championed on the grounds of abolishing the slave trade. After Britain annexed Ashanti, the issue of human sacrifices was used as propaganda for the invasion. Hobson's explanation of the success of this propaganda is pertinent to the current discussion.

Hobson noted that a section of society possessed a 'genuine desire to spread Christianity among the heathen, to diminish the cruelty and other sufferings which they believe exist in countries less fortunate than their own, and do good work about the world in the cause of humanity'. Hobson saw how the assumption of moral superiority invited intervention:

> Ill-trained for the most part in psychology and history, these people believe that religion and other arts of civilization are portable commodities which it is our duty to convey to the backward nations, and that a certain amount of compulsion is justified in pressing their benefits upon people too ignorant at once to recognize them.

What Hobson sketched out is the standpoint of moral imperialism. Here, humanitarian sentiment is directed towards protecting people from themselves.

The relationship that Hobson drew between moral and material interests was a subtle one:

> Is it surprising that the selfish forces which direct Imperialism should utilize the protective colours of these disinterested movements? Imperialist politicians, soldiers, or company directors, who push a forward policy by portraying the cruelties of the African slave raids or the infamous tyranny of a Prempeh or a Theebaw, or who open out a new field for missionary enterprise in China or the Soudan, do not deliberately and consciously work up these motives in order to incite the British public. They simply and instinctively attach themselves to any strong, genuine elevated feeling which is of service, fan it and feed it until it assumes fervour, and utilize it for their ends.[32]

In other words the existing moral and humanitarian concerns provide a vocabulary through which the imperialist dynamic can be expressed. What is crucial here is the existence of the assumption of moral superiority, which endows the West with the ability to provide a solution to others problems. From this perspective it is possible to see how the imperial mission happily reconciled material self-interest with a self-flattering moral framework.

Hobson's insights have considerable relevance to the situation today. The moral rehabilitation of imperialism could not succeed without a significant humanitarian input from liberal-minded sections of Western societies. That is why issues like Third World famines have been so important in the construction of a climate of opinion in which it is seen as self-evident that the West has the solution. Events like Live Aid and other global charity initiatives have done more than anything to popularise the view that Third World people need to be looked after and protected, not least from themselves.

The motives and idealism of many Western youth and aid volunteers are not in question. Unfortunately whatever their motives, in practice their moral sentiments have been mobilised to assist Western diplomacy. The very language used reflects this symbiotic relationship. For example, until recently Western eugenic policies towards the Third World were described as 'population control'. Today such policies are more likely to be conveyed in liberal, politically correct language. Population control is sold on the basis of 'empowering women' or of giving women rights. According to the British Overseas Development Administration (ODA), their aim is to create a climate in which 'couples can exercise reproductive choice'.[33] Presumably the choice of having lots more children is not the one that the ODA has in mind.

The emphasis on humanitarian themes is central to the rehabilitation of imperialism. There is a need both to rehabilitate imperialism's past and to dissociate it from the negative images that have dogged it in the postwar period. Feuer has directly addressed this problem by attempting artificially to separate the Nazi experience from the dynamic of imperialism: 'The experience of the Nazi species of imperialism, with its intellectual and emotional trauma, has perhaps misdirected many thinkers into supposing that anti-Semitism and racism arise from an inherent dynamic of imperialism.'[34]

Today there is even a tendency to separate the nationalist passion of imperialism from Western intervention. There is a self-conscious attempt to project intervention in a multilateral or international form. So United Nations resolutions are routinely deployed to legitimise *force majeure*. The UN troops in Somalia or Cambodia are described not as what they really are – an army of occupation – but as 'peace-keeping' forces involved in 'humanitarian' tasks, usually in opposition to Third World 'warlords'. From this standpoint major military operations can be depicted as acts of disinterested generosity by a reluctant Western power.

Contemporary Anti Third World Themes

The emerging culture of imperialism has developed through the projection of a range of anti Third World themes. Many of the motifs are reminiscent of the arguments used to demonise Third World nation-alism, as discussed previously. But since the Third World already stands morally discredited, the emphasis now is on establishing a coherent Western identity. Western societies find it difficult to generate a positive vision on their own account. There are few obvious sources of legitimacy that can be tapped by Western governments. Economic depression, political stagnation and social malaise mean that there is no dynamic towards the creation of a positive national identity in Western capitalist nations.

In these circumstances, Western politicians seek to gain moral authority through highlighting their relationship with other morally 'inferior' societies. That is why failed politicians who are unable to solve the problems of inner-city London or downtown New York feel so much more comfortable with handling the situation in Mogadishu with a few helicopter gunships. In contrast to its failures at home, the West seems always to triumph abroad.

However, the very success of anti Third World ideology exposes its inner weakness. The tension between the West's domestic malaise and its lofty moral pretensions abroad cannot be submerged indefinitely. The sense that things are out of control at home must create confusion about imperial adventures abroad. The attempt to displace domestic problems on to the international plane creates a situation where sooner or later the profound underlying insecurities become exposed.

The invocation of the 'Third World Threat' has now become habitual in Western discourse. Increasingly the dimensions of this threat have been overstretched to such an extent that it serves mainly to reveal the West's own insecurity and lack of confidence about itself. The fear within is focused on to the supposed threat from without.

The threat of Third World terrorism has recently been supplemented by a variety of new threats: the threat of nuclear proliferation, envi-ronmental terrorisms, the danger of the drug trade, the rise of fundamentalism, and the peril of overpopulation and migration. The unrestrained Western reaction against the Third World is so pervasive that even so-called non-military problems have been recruited to sustain the siege mentality. One writer even holds out the prospect of 'non-military conflicts in the field of demography, environment or health'. According to this Social-Darwinist scenario, 'Europe is increasingly confronted with the so-called "threats of the twenty-first century": AIDS, drugs, pollution, and the proliferation of chemical and biological weapons in the Third World'.[35] The preoccupation with such Malthusian themes of survival exposes the all pervasive social-pessimism in this discussion.

Discussions of the Third World tend to take the form of a shopping-list of threats, exemplified by the the term 'threats of the twenty-first century'. One contributor to the *Journal of International Affairs* warns of 'unfamiliar new dangers' such as the possibility of the collapse of China or India, the 'rise of post-modern nationalism' and the 'revival of religious fundamentalism'.[36] The deliberations on this subject are often thin on facts. Vague generalisation allows maximum scope for inflating a problem and transforming it into a 'threat'.

The threat of Third World nuclear capability – sometimes called the 'Islamic Bomb' – is a case in point. Any state can be branded as a nuclear threat, without the slightest attempt at substantiating the accusation. According to the Stockholm Research Institute for Studies of Conflict and Terrorism, there was no evidence of Iraq's nuclear potential at the time of the Gulf War. Yet the world was led to believe that it had been saved in the nick of time from Saddam's nuclear holocaust. The literature on this subject is so irrational that anything goes. Two American writers suggested that even relatively poor African states could become a nuclear threat since soon 'it will be possible to duplicate almost all past technology in all but the most forlorn Third World backwaters'.[37] There does not need to be a nuclear bomb for the construction of a threat. As Barry Buzan argued, 'the concern over Iraq, Libya, Israel, Pakistan, South Africa, Brazil and other states has as much to do with their industrialization as with their direct imports of arms'.[38] The possession of an industrial base, once considerd a step forward, is now enough for a Third World state to be considered a threat to world peace.

Nuclear terrorists have been joined by drug dealers in the West's rogues gallery: 'Now that communist guerillas are on the wane, the US military is training Latin forces to battle drug traffickers, the new enemy.'[39] The invention of the Third World drug threat is even more absurd than the contributions on nuclear proliferation. It conveniently ignores that the market for drugs, like the international arms bazaar, was created not by Bolivian peasants but by Western entrepreneurs. It also conveniently overlooks the CIA's role in internationalising the drug trade through its covert activities in south-east Asia. But above all the very premise of the threat is false. The problem of drugs has the label 'Made in the West' stamped all over it. It is a symptom of the social malaise that afflicts Western societies, to which cocaine farmers in Peru are entirely incidental.

In the United States and Europe the campaign against Third World threats is increasingly translated into a crusade to keep foreigners out. As an unsigned article in the American *National Review* proposed, 'in simple language: keep out terrorists trying to come in; throw out those already here; and hit hard at the foreign states sponsoring them'.[40] 'Terrorists' become any foreign people you don't like. Moreover terrorism is redefined to serve as an all-purpose metaphor for the Third World, demanding concerted action from the West. So a recent report by the Trilateral Commission warns that international migration, with its connections to such issues as environmental degradation, drugs and terrorism, is a 'new fact of national and international life that requires cooperation of all kinds among all nations'.[41]

The explosion of irrational fears suggests that the West feels less than secure about its own survival. The threat of the Third World nuclear bomb has been supplemented by the peril posed by the 'population time-bomb'. The current discussion on Third World population growth has assumed grotesque proportions. Kishore Mahbubani writes that in the past geographic distance would have insulated the West from the teeming masses of the Third World but now technology has changed all that. The invasion of Third World immigrants will overwhelm the West unless some action is taken.[42]

The discussion on the population explosion and the threat of hordes of Third World people invading the West displays the strong cultural and racial themes that have long underpinned the demonisation of Third World nationalism. It is important to note that the exploding population in question is always non-Western. Consequently the discussion of population and immigration is intimately linked to cultural – and, implicitly, racial – issues. According to Buzan:

> In combination, migration threats and the clash of cultures make it rather easy to draw a scenario for a kind of societal Cold War between the centre and at least part of the periphery and specifically between the West and Islam, in which Europe would be in the front line.[43]

Another contributor to this discussion warns of how the 'religious-political conflicts' of North Africa are 'likely to be played out, or at least reflected, in Paris and other big French cities'.[44] Such contributions have so far tended to stop just short of a call for a new Crusade.

Predictably, the panic-like reaction to population growth and migration is often conveyed in an anti-Islamic mode. This is especially the case with the popular media. So, for example, an editorial in a popular daily published in Strasbourg warned that the main 'weapon' of Islamic fundamentalists was now demography.[45] The shift towards demographic themes creates a situation in which the West, rather than being the aggressive invader in the Third World, becomes the target of alien invasion. One conservative American contributor gave voice to this sentiment when he concluded that 'protecting Western culture from foreign assault requires domestic revival'. He added, 'the twenty-first century could once again find Islam at the gates of Vienna, as immigrants or terrorists if not as armies'.[46] This defensive posture suggests that the crisis of confidence of the Anglo-American political elite continues to influence its perception of the Third World.

The defensiveness is clearly focused on the theme of threatened Western values. The revival of themes associated with Spengler suggests that the recent success in morally rehabilitating imperialism has not been enough to overcome the intellectual and ideological crisis of the Anglo-American elites. The spotlight is once again on resentment, and rejection of the West. Conservative intellectuals, particularly in America, are obsessed with the threat to Western culture. For example, William Lind proposes that 'for conservatives, the goal should be clear: the defense of Western culture abroad as at home'. Lind's reaction to the apparent threats to Western culture is positively irrational. 'In Latin America, there is a real possibility of a marriage between the drug business and anti-Western ideology', he argues. His concern with Incan 'revivalism' betrays more about Lind's preoccupation than real relations of power.

It is not only conservative contributors who have taken on the theme of cultural survival. Written from a liberal perspective, Paul Kennedy's *Preparing For the Twenty-First Century* offers a coherent synthesis of the cultural and Malthusian strands of arguments. Kennedy, in line with other contributors, stresses the decline of the population of the West in relation to other societies. For Kennedy, this development has:

> raised the interesting question of whether 'Western values' – a liberal social culture, human rights, religious tolerance, democracy, market forces – will maintain their prevailing position in a world overwhelmingly peopled by societies which did not experience the rational scientific and liberal assumptions of the Enlightenment.[47]

This is a more delicate way of posing the issue of Western survival. As an aside it is worth noting that values associated with the Enlightenment, and therefore with a universalist outlook, are here presented in the particularist form of 'Western values'. It also reveals a lot about an intellectual outlook which sees the *survival of a value* as predicated on the numbers of people living in 'rational' societies, rather than on its intrinsic merits.

The evolution of anti Third World ideology towards crude demography has important consequences. It means that the Third World no longer has to do anything to constitute a threat. Simply through the elementary act of reproduction, Third World peoples now threaten Western culture and societies. The implications of this perspective, implications which are seldom spelt out, is dramatic. The problem is no longer focused on a single terrorist, or a group of malcontent anti-colonial nationalists, or a particular regime or even a whole religion like Islam. The problem is the Third World as such, engaged in the act of life and reproduction. This is in effect a new hi-tech Social-Darwinism, backed by the power of western militarism, waiting for a mission.

Reflections on the Moral Rehabilitation of Imperialism

An exploration of the changing Western perceptions of the societies of Africa and Asia during this century helps to situate the strong fears and passions that dominate this subject. Just as the Anglo-American elite experienced anti-colonial nationalism as a challenge to its legitimacy, so its perceptions of contemporary Third World reactions are guided by similar passions, only more so. Until the 1940s these themes were the domain of specialists. Occasionally a contribution like Spengler's *Decline of the West* would reach a wider audience. But the obsession with the threat from the colonies was a secondary motif within the Anglo-American political culture. Today, the issues discussed in this chapter are at the centre of Western political discourse. International relations specialists, journalists and government officials tend broadly to agree that, in one shape or another, the Third World constitutes the main threat to global stability.

At first sight the intense emotion with which Third World threats are discussed seems slightly ironic. After all, the age of anti-colonialism has ended, giving way to an era in which demoralisation has overwhelmed anti-imperialists. As argued above, the West has recovered some of the moral ground that it lost previously. The anti Third World ideology of the 1960s and 1970s could discredit its target but not renew a positive identification with the West. In the 1980s and 1990s, however, it has gone a step further towards the latter objective. The post Cold War military adventures in Iraq and Somalia indicate that there is now a formidable consensus in the West supporting military intervention. The right of the West to intervene in and determine the life of other societies is now accepted by significant sections of American and European society.

However, the attempt to rehabilitate imperialism may be a case of too little and too late. The experience of history shows that it is difficult to recapture the moment that is lost. The very act of rehabilitation implies the recognition of the defects that caused the problems in the first place. After all, rehabilitation would not be necessary if imperialism were unproblematic. Today, a positive culture of imperialism could have only a limited impact, because it is not the organic product of contemporary society. The imperialist political culture that so inspired the Anglo-American elite a century ago evolved at a time when imperialism was in the ascendancy, a time of economic strength and optimism in Western society. The late twentieth century is conspicuously different to the era of imperialist ascendancy. The new culture of imperialism lacks the robust vitality of Victorian capitalism. It is a culture that can serve to *console* but not to *inspire*.

Seen in this light, it is hardly surprising that the moral rehabilitation of imperialism is far from secure. Fears about Western culture indicate just how the situation has changed. During the rise of imperialism, confidence in the superiority of Western culture was all pervasive. American and British imperialists had no fears of losing the initiative to other cultures. Today, the insecure musings about a 'clash of culture' and panics about the spread of Islam underline the problem of legitimacy in Western societies. These insecurities give Western attitudes towards Third World societies an irrational and unpredictable character. It seems that in the very act of settling scores with the Third World, the worst fears of the West about its own transience have been confirmed.

The new culture of imperialism lacks the relatively stable bases of the old. As a result, the actions of Western powers in the world are more unstable and potentially more dangerous than previously. Unfortunately the moral credibility which Western intervention has acquired at home means that these dangers are not widely perceived today. Even relatively critically-minded people in Europe and America are apt to accept that tiny, technologically insignificant countries like Libya are a greater threat to the world then the powerful Western capitalist nations. The aim of this book is to question that consensus. Unless such questions are asked, there will be nothing restraining the new imperialists from acting out their 'clash of cultures' nightmares by turning the world into a battlefield.

Notes and References

Chapter 1: Introduction

1. J.J. Mearsheimer, 'Why We Will Soon Miss The Cold War', *The Atlantic Monthly*, August 1990.
2. *Sunday Times,* 11 March 1990.
3. See *Newsweek*, 21 June 1993; *The Times*, 28 August 1990; *Daily Telegraph*, 3 February 1993; and *Sunday Telegraph*, 7 February 1993.
4. J. Lukacs, 'The End of the Twentieth Century', *Harper's Magazine*, January 1993 and Fukuyama (1992).
5. C. Krautheimer, 'The Unipolar Moment', *Foreign Affairs,* vol. 70, no. 4, 1990/1991, p.31; and C. Layne, 'Realism Redux: Strategic Independence in a Multipolar World', *SAISS Review*, vol. 9, no. 2, 1989, p. 22.
6. See B. Buzan, 'New Patterns of Global Security', *International Affairs*, July 1991, p. 449.
7. S.P. Huntington, 'The Clash of Civilisations?', *Foreign Affairs*, Summer 1993, pp. 22, 31 and 49.
8. Gurtov (1974) p. 2.
9. Kohn (1932) p. 63.
10. Griswold (1966) p. 247.
11. Kohn (1932) p. 21.
12. Mayall (1990) p. 47.
13. See R.H. Jackson, 'Juridical Statehood in Africa', *Journal of International Affairs*, vol. 46, no. 1, 1992, pp. 3–4.
14. R. Lynd, 'Preface' to Dryhurst (1919) p. vii.
15. S.K. Ratcliffe, 'Aspects of the Social Movement in India', *The Sociological Review*, vol. 1, no. 4, 1908, pp. 373–5.
16. N.J. Spykman, 'The Social Background of Asiatic Nationalism', *American Journal of Sociology*, vol. 32, 1926–7, p. 406.
17. See Ginsberg (1964) p. 31 and Arendt (1967) pp. 160–6.
18. On this process, see the path-breaking study of Hroch (1985).
19. Gurtov (1974) p. 2.
20. Tidrick (1990) p. 223.
21. See E.G. Colvin, 'The Changing Scene In India', *The Nineteenth Century*, September 1919, p. 445.
22. This pamphlet 'The Burmese Situation 1930–31', can be found in the India Office Registry and Library (IOR) *L/P&J/6/2020*.
23. Furnivall (1948) pp. 142 and 197.

24. Hodgkin (1957) p. 21.
25. Rosebery (1900) pp. 5, 11 and 13.
26. Lansing (1921) p. 97.

Chapter 2: A Presentiment of Danger

1. Snyder (1939) pp. 281 and 291.
2. Matthews (1926) p. 93.
3. A.L.P. Dennis, 'Exploitation of Underdeveloped Areas' in Turner (1923) pp. 29–30.
4. Laski (1932) p. 42.
5. Westermann (1939) p. 304.
6. W.O. Brown, 'Race Consciousness Among South African Natives', *American Journal of Sociology*, vol. 40, 1935, p. 581.
7. Malinowski (1938), p. xxxv.
8. Hughes and Hughes (1981 reprint) p. 47.
9. A. Mazrui, 'Africa Entrapped: Between the Protestant Ethic and the Legacy of Westphalia', in H. Bull and A. Watson eds: *The Expansion of International Society*, Oxford, 1984, p. 297.
10. See R. Headrick, 'African Soldiers in World War II', *Armed Forces and Society*, vol. 4, no. 3, Spring 1978, p. 501 and D. Killingray, 'Ex-Servicemen in the Gold Coast', *The Journal of Modern African Studies*, vol. 21, no.3., 1983, p. 533.
11. See for example E.P.A. Schleh, 'The Post-War careers of Ex-Servicemen in Ghana and Uganda', *The Journal of Modern African Studies*, vol. 6, no. 2, 1968.
12. Public Record Office, Kew Gardens (PRO): *INF 1/559*, 'Plan of propaganda to British West Africa. Addendum to Appreciation. Paper no. 513 A', 6 September 1944.
13. Arthur Creech-Jones, 'British Colonial Policy', *International Affairs*, April 1951, p. 176.
14. PRO: *CO 968/22/5*, 'Extract from a semi-official letter from Sir Philip Mitchell, Governor of Fiji, to Mr. Gent, dated 5 August 1943'.
15. See PRO: *CO 968/78/11*, 'Stanley Oliver to Rt Hon. Sir William Jowitt', 13 November 1943 and *INF 1/554*, 'Minute from HV Usill', 4 October 1943.
16. PRO: *CO 968/78/11*, 'Oliver to Sir William Jowitt', 13 November 1943.
17. For an example of this issues raised in this discussion, see R. Fane, 'The return of the Soldier; East Africa', *Journal of the Royal African Society*, vol. 43, no. 171, April 1948.
18. See Capt. A.G. Dickson, 'An Experiment in Mass Education, Report on the Nyasaland and Northern Rhodesia Tour of the (EA) Mobile Propaganda Unit', enclosed in 'Dickson to Lord Lugard', 8 March 1943 in Box 36, Papers of the International Africa Institute (IAI) held at the London School of Economics.

19. See PRO: *CO 875/8/8*, 'Mobile propaganda Safari in Uganda' enclosure to H.C.G. Gurney, Nairobi to G.F. Seal, Colonial Office, 17 May 1943.

20. See Headrick *op. cit.*, p. 514 and E.E. Sabben-Claire: 'African Troops in Asia', *African Affairs*, vol. 44, no. 177, October 1945, p. 157.

21. PRO: *CO 852/588/11*, 'Cabinet Memorandum by the Secretary of State for the Colonies', 15 November 1944.

22. See PRO: *Inf 1/554*, 'H.V. Usill, MOI to Sir G. Northcote, Principal Information Officer, East Africa', 7 October 1943 and *INF 1/559*, 'Overseas Planning Committee. Paper 513, Plan of Propaganda to British West Africa', 3 July 1944.

23. National Archives and Records Administration, Washington, DC: *RG 59 848N.401/10–1945*, 'T.A. Hickok, American Consul, Accra to Secretary of State for the Colonies', 18 October 1945.

24. *The Times*, 21 August 1947.

25. PRO: *CO 536/215*, 'Governor of Uganda to Colonial Secretary', 9 January 1946.

26. PRO: *CO 536/215*, 'Governor of Uganda to Secretary of State for the Colonies', 11 May 1946.

27. PRO: *WO 269/1*, 'HQ, E. Af. Command, Nairobi Circular to officers', 11 July 1946.

28. See PRO: *WO 269/2*, 'HQ, E. Af. Command for Distribution. Appendix A. Notes on Possible Causes and Types of Unrest', 9 November 1946 and 'L.Col. Irwen for distribution' 18 November 1946.

29. PRO: *CO 968/11/7*, 'Minute by W.L. Rolleston to Mr. Calder', 20 February 1942.

30. Cited in K.W. Grundy, 'Racial and Ethnic Relations in the Armed Forces', *Armed Forces and Society*, vol. 2, no. 2, Winter 1976, p. 227.

31. See for example those cited in Headrick *op. cit.*, pp. 511–14 and A.M. Israel, 'Measuring the War Experience: Ghananian Soldiers in World War II', *The Journal of Modern African Studies*, 25, 1, 1987, pp. 162–4.

32. IOR: *L/WS/1/567*, 'Cipher Telegram. War Office to Commander in Chief, India', 13 March 1945.

33. See PRO: *CO 968/92/2*, 'Minute by A.H. Poynton', 20 September 1943.

34. Cited in A. Palmer, 'Black American Soldiers in Trinidad 1942–1943', *10th Conference of Caribbean Historians*, Nassau, Bahamas, April 1986, p. 5.

35. PRO: *CO 968/92/2*, 'Telegram. Secretary of State for the Colonies to Resident Minister, Accra', 29 September 1943.

36. *Ibid*.

37. PRO: *CO 968/78/13*, 'Minute by TK Lloyd to Gent', 25 August 1942.

38. Raymond Firth, 'Social Problems and Research in British West Africa', *Africa*, vol. 17, no. 2, April 1947, p. 80.

39. Kohn (1932) p. 62.

40. This point is well argued by Grundy in relation to South Africa. On the official sensitivity towards 'race and ethnic questions' in the military see Grundy *op. cit.*, p. 228,

41. See Schleh, *op. cit.*, p. 206.
42. See Headrick, *op. cit.*, p. 511.
43. PRO: *PREM 11/3665*, 'Prime Minister Harold Macmillan to Prime Minister Robert Menzies', 15 January 1962.
44. These points are developed further in F. Füredi: *Mythical Past, Elusive Future*, London, 1992, pp. 141–52.
45. PRO: *CO 137/887*, 'Extract of Note of Meeting of Jamaica's Attorney General Mayers with the Secretary of State', 5 August 1949.
46. See G.O. Olusanya, 'The Role of Ex-Servicemen in Nigerian Politics', *The Journal of Modern African Studies*, vol. 6, no. 2, 1968, p. 224.
47. See Echenberg (1991) p. 106, Malan is cited by Grundy (1983) p. 92.
48. Cited by C. Fyfe, 'Review of *The Labour Government and the End of Empire*', *Race and Class*, vol. 33, no. 4, p. 103.

Chapter 3: The Social Construction of the Third World Terrorist

1. For a discussion of the role of the Mahdiyya movement, see Morsy (1984) pp. 247–66.
2. See Fanon (1970) pp. 53 and 89.
3. Mockaitis (1990) p. 1.
4. Ibid. p. 12.
5. See Low, 'The End of the British Empire in Africa' in Gifford and Louis (1988) p. 63, Mockaitis (1990) p. 12 and Tidrick (1990) p. 2.
6. Laski (1932) p. 38.
7. See *Manchester Guardian*, 30 December 1930 and 21 August 1931.
8. *Manchester Guardian*, 29 December 1930 and 2 February 1931 and *Daily Telegraph*, 1 January 1931.
9. See Department of State, Intelligence Report no. 6307, *The Mau Mau: An Aggressive Reaction to Frustration*, 12 June 1953, Washington D.C.
10. Nye (1975) p. 62.
11. Le Bon (1990) p. 110.
12. *Daily Mail*, 18 January 1991.
13. See Ostrogorski (1902) , Lowell (1913) and Michels (1949).
14. Ginsberg (1964) p. 114.
15. See for example: A.V. Dicey, *Lectures on the Relation Between Law and Public Opinion in England During the Nineteenth Century*, 1905; A.L. Lowell, *Public Opinion and Popular Government*, 1913; and W. Lipman, *Public Opinion*, 1922.
16. See Lippman, *op. cit.*, p. 75 and E.H. Paget, 'Sudden Changes in Group Opinion', *Social Forces*, vol. 7, no. 3, March 1929, p. 439.
17. Hobson (1901) p. 9.
18. Wallas (1961) (originally published 1908) p. 243.
19. Lipset (1963) p. 82.
20. Cited in Nye, *op. cit*, p. 51.
21. Bagehot (1872) p. 117.

22. Perham (1962) p. 114.
23. Wallas, *op. cit.*, p. 289.
24. Hayes (1926) p. 278.
25. Hobson (1988) p. 4.
26. Laski (1932) p. 43.
27. See RIIA (1939) pp. xiv and 186, and (1937) p. 3.
28. Namier (1962) and Bullock (1991) p. 1072.
29. E. Marmarstein, 'The Fate of Arabdom: A Study on Comparative Nationalism', *International Affairs*, vol. 25, October 1949, p. 490.
30. Kohn (1946) p. 543.
31. PRO: *CO 537/2677*, 'East Africa Political Intelligence Report', July–September 1948.
32. PRO: *FO 953/1530*. 'P1011/3. FO Paper: South East Asia', 3 December 1954.
33. Myrdal (1960) pp. 2111, 2117 and 2118.
34. J. Plamenatz, 'Two Types of Nationalism' in Kamemka (1976) pp. 33–4 and Smith (1991) p. 11.
35. Fukuyama (1992) p. xx.
36. See E.H. Carr (1941) p. 36. Lord Milverton, 'Thoughts on Nationalism in Africa', *Corona*, December 1955, p. 445.
37. Walsby (1947) p. 64, Popper (1952) p. 244 and Stern (1974) p. xv.
38. See PRO: *FO 953/254*, 'Burma Historical Background', 5 February 1948, '"Z": Argentina in the Tunnel', *Foreign Affairs*, no. 3, vol. 30, April 1952, p. 391, PRO: *FO 371/56786*, 'Minute by R. Murray', 16 August 1946.
39. Crocker (1949) p. 112.
40. PRO: *CO 537/2450*, 'OC Noel to the High Commissioner for the Western Pacific', 11 August 1947.
41. Cited in PRO: *DO 35/5357*, 'VC Martin, Office of the High Commission, New Delhi to RC Ormerod, CRO', 1 September 1953.
42. P. Abrahams, 'The Conflict of Culture in Africa', *International Affairs*, July 1954, p. 307.
43. The most significant exception to this trend was the American cultural relativist school. For a more sympathetic treatment of the emerging African response to colonialism see Herskovits (1967) (originally published in 1941).
44. For example Melville Herskovits', *The Myth of the Negro Past*, originally published in 1941, treats 'Africanism' or what would later be called black nationalism not only as inevitable but also as a positive phenomenon.
45. Malinowski (1938) p. xxxv.
46. Evans-Pritchard (1965) p. 105. The exaggeration of differences is particularly striking in the treatment of the pre-colonial past. See Hammond and Jablow (1970).
47. M. Fortes, 'An Anthropologist's Point of View', in Hinden (1944) pp. 221–2.

48. R. Linton, 'Nativistic Movements', *American Anthropologist*, vol. 45, 1943, p. 230.

49. Said (1985) p. 236.

50. C.H. Allan, 'Marching Rule: A Nativistic Cult of the British Solomon Islands', *Corona*, March 1951, p. 97.

51. See Malinowski (1938) p. xiv.

52. E. Huxley, 'The Rise of the African Zealot', *Corona*, May 1950, p. 2.

53. Allan, 'Marching Rule …', p. 96.

54. PRO: *WO269/8*, HQ, EAfCmnd., 'The Defence, in Peacetime, of East Africa Command', 8 June 1948.

55. PRO: *CO 936/217*, 'The Problem of Nationalism' enclosure 'W. Strang, Foreign Office, to T.K. Lloyd, Colonial Office, 21 June 1952.

56. PRO: *FO 953/1530*, P1011/3. FO Paper 'South East Asia. Part 1. Information Policy', 3 December 1954.

57. Richmond (1955) p. 192.

58. Toynbee (1948) pp. 207–8.

59. Cited in C.S.L. Chachage, 'British Rule and African Civilization in Tanganyika', *Journal of Historical Sociology*, vol. 1, no. 2, June 1988, p. 217.

60. Stonequist (1961) p. 50, originally published in 1931.

61. Said *op. cit.* p. 249.

62. R.E. Park, 'Human Migration and the Marginal Man', *American Journal of Sociology*, vol. 33, 1928, p. 893.

63. For Durkheim *moral anomie* represented the key threat to social stability. See Durkheim (1964) pp. 1–4.

64. PRO: *FO 953/1230*, 'Information Secretary, British Embassy, Teheran to Eastern Department, Foreign Office', 16 June 1952.

65. M. Fortes, 'An Anthropologist's Point of View', Hinden (1944) p. 225.

66. Richmond (1955) p. 25.

67. Malinowski (1945) pp. 60–1.

68. See L.H. Palmer, 'Indonesia and the West', *International Affairs*, April 1955, pp. 183–4, and M.R. Masani, 'The Mind of Asia', *Foreign Affairs*, vol. 33, no. 4, July 1955, p. 555.

69. E.B. Mitford, 'Cause and Effect in India', *The Fortnightly Review*, July–December 1919, p. 131.

70. Mayo (1927) p. 28.

71. PRO: *CO 927/170/3*, 'A.I. Richards to P. Rogers', 14 March 1952.

72. PRO: *CO/847/25/7*, 'Factors Affecting Native Administration Policy', by G.B. Cartland, January 1946.

Chapter 4: From Containment to Accommodation

1. Hammond and Jablow (1970) p. 115.

2. PRO: *INF 12/303*, 'COI: Far East Publicity Committee – Minutes', 13 March 1950.

3. See Buell (1965) vol. 1, p. 376, originally published in 1928.

4. Snyder (1989) p. 280.

5. Staniland (1991) p. 23.

6. J.S. Coleman, 'Nationalism in Tropical Africa', *American Political Science Review*, vol. 48, 1954, p. 404.

7. See IOR: *M-3-476*, 'Oxford University Summer School in Colonial Administration. Second Session – 1938', p. 61.

8. NARA: *RG59 611.70/2-2350*, 'P.N. Jester, Consul General, Dakar, to Department of State', 15 February 1950.

9. See PRO: *CO/968/5/9*, 'Minute by T.K. Lloyd' 12 March 1942, and 'Sir C. Dundas to G. Gater, Colonial Office', 4 March 1943. *CO 583/277/30658/46*, 'Sir A. Richards to Rt. Hon. George Hall', 9 August 1946.

10. PRO: *CO 875/75/1*, 'Governor, Sierra Leone to Sir C. Jeffries', 31 December 1949.

11. PRO: *CO 536/215*, 'Enclosure to Governor of Uganda to A. Creech-Jones', 11 May 1946.

12. Cartland, 'Factors affecting …', *op. cit.*

13. Rhodes House Library (RHL) : *Papers of Arthur Creech-Jones, Box 55/4*, 'Governor P. Mitchell to A. Creech-Jones', 16 September 1948.

14. 'Indirect Rule in West Africa', *The Round Table*, vol. 39, December 1948, p. 126.

15. Macmillan (1949) p. 285.

16. Jester, *op. cit.*

17. PRO: *CO 537/5263*, 'A Survey of Communism in Africa', by Research Department, Foreign Office, August 1950.

18. PRO: *CO 936/217*, See 'Problem of Nationalism', *op. cit.* in 'W. Strang, FO to T.K. Lloyd', 21 June 1952.

19. Lord Hailey, 'Nationalism in Africa', *Journal of the Royal African Society*, vol. 36, no. 143, April 1937, pp. 146 and 147.

20. See PRO: *CO 852/1053/1*, 'Opening address to the Summer conference' by A. Creech-Jones, 19 August 1948.

21. Office of Strategic Services; *Nationalist Trends in British West Africa*, R and A no. 2279, Washington, DC, 1944, p. 22.

22. NARA: *RG 59 848N. 401/10-1945*, 'A. Hickok to Secretary of State', 19 October 1945.

23. PRO: *INF 1/559*, 'Minute from the M.O.I. Representative to the Resident Minister of State', 3 July 1944.

24. For a report on the differences expressed at the Cambridge school see NARA: *RG59 848N.01.8-647*, 'John Palmer, 2nd Acting Chief, Division of African Affairs to E. Talbot Smith, Accra Consulate', 8 June 1947.

25. NARA: *RG59 848A.00/10-1245*, 'T. Holcomb, American Legation, Pretoria to Secretary of State', 12 October 1945.

26. NARA: *RG59 848T.00/8-B4G*, 'J.L. Touchette, American Consul, Nairobi, to Secretary of State', 8 August 1946.

27. The American Consul in Dakar observed 'many signs of a growing racial and economic self-consciousness'. See NARA: *RG59 851T.00/12-545*, 'J.R. Wilkinson to Secretary of State', 5 December 1945.

28. See NARA: *RG59 848K.00*, 'British Colonies Of West Africa. Policy and Information Statement'. 12 December 1946.

29. Noer (1988) p. 17.

30. NARA: *RG59 711.5/N/1-2847*, 'Office Memorandum. C. Timberlake to Mr. Henderson', 28 January 1948.

31. NARA: *RG 59 n.00*, 'E. Talbot Smith, Accra to Secretary of State', 2 June 1948.

32. See Dean Acheson's request for information on this subject in NARA: *RG59 845K.062/3-150*, 15 March 1950.

33. PRO: *PREM 8/923*, 'Memorandum by Arthur Creech-Jones', 6 January 1948.

34. PRO: *CO 537/4402*, 'Minute by A Creech-Jones', October 1948.

35. Bradley (1966) p. 151.

36. PRO: *CO 936/217*, 'W.G. Wilson minute', 4 July 1952.

37. These points are discussed at length in Füredi (1994) Chapter 7.

38. PRO: *CO 554/254*, 'Lloyd to Sir John Macpherson', 5 March 1953.

39. PRO: *CO 822/1430*, 'Minute by Sir J. Macpherson', 19 August 1957.

40. McGhee (1983) p. 114.

41. NARA: *RG59 745H.00/4-2351*, 'E.H. Bourgerie circular to Consulates in Africa', 23 April 1951.

42. Cited in Noer, *op. cit.*, p. 30.

43. See for example NARA: *RG59 511.45K/10-1751*, 'H. Bloom, American Consul, Accra to Department of State', 17 October 1951.

44. NARA: *RG 59 511.45K5/4-251*, 'H. Bloom to Department of State', 2 April 1951.

45. NARA: *RG59 770.00/9-2050SF*, 'Summary of discussion held at the Foreign Office on the 20th of September 1950'.

46. NARA: *RG59 511.45K/11-3051*, 'J.R. Bartelt, Jr., American Consulate, Accra to The Department of State', 30 November 1951.

47. This point is elaborated in detail in Füredi, *Colonial Wars and the Politics of Third World Nationalism* (1994).

48. PRO: *CO 822/1430*, 'W.L. Gorell Barnes to Sir J. Macpherson', 20 August 1957.

49. PRO: *CO 537/5263*, 'A Survey of ...' *op. cit.*

50. Hailey (1957) p. 251.

51. See PRO: *CO 879/137*, *op. cit.*

52. Department of State: *Africa a Special Assessment*, Intelligence Report 7103, 3 January 1956.

53. NARA: *RG59 745p. 00/12-3055*, 'E.J. Dorsz to Department of State', 30 December 1955.

54. NARA: *RG 59 611.45p/12-754*, 'E.J. Dorsz, Nairobi to Department of State', 7 December 1954.
55. See for example the discussion in PRO: *CO 859/1150* regarding American meddling in labour affairs in Africa.
56. PRO: *CO 936/576*, 'Pan African Conference. Foreign Office INTEL no. 88', 16 May 1957.
57. *Daily Telegraph*, 12 November 1957.
58. PRO: *FO 371/137945*, 'J.H.A. Watson, FO to ACE Malcolm, Tunis', 10 June 1959.
59. PRO: *CO 936/570*, 'The Political Scene in Tropical Africa', Research Department, Foreign Office, November 1958.
60. Both Eisenhower and Elbrick cited in Mahoney (1983) p. 35.
61. R.A. Scalapino, '"Neutralism" in Asia', *American Political Science Review*, vol. 48. 1954, p. 49.
62. Enclosure to 'P.L. Carter, British Embassy, Washington to G.F.N. Reddaway, Information Research Department (FO)' 29 March 1958 in PRO: *CO 936/576*.
63. 'Minute from H.T.B. Smith', 16 April 1958 in ibid.
64. 'Carter to Reddaway' in ibid.
65. PRO: *FO371/137994*, 'S.A. Lockhart to K.M. Wilford, FO' 17 August 1959.
66. *Daily Telegraph*, 29 July 1954.
67. See PRO: *PREM 11/2587*, 'Macmillan to Secretary of State for Foreign Affairs', 28 July 1959.
68. *Daily Express*, 15 July 1960.

Chapter 5: Imperialism on the Defensive

1. F.S. Meyer, 'The Prickly Dilemmas' in Meyer (1965) p. 28.
2. PRO: *PREM 11/3665*, 'H. Macmillan to R. Menzies', 9 February 1962.
3. Taylor 'Patriotism, History...', p. 974.
4. *Daily Express*, 21 October 1949.
5. Fitzgerald (1979) p. 55.
6. See PRO: *FO953/136*, 'A.A. Dudley to K.W. Blackburne' 28 June 1948.
7. Burns (1957) p. 73.
8. See Crocker (1947) p. 108, Burns (1957) p. 5 and V. Harlow, 'Our Challenge to Communism from the Political Point of View', *Corona*, August 1951.
9. Cited in Porter and Stockwell (1989) p. 153.
10. PRO: *CO875/19/3*. 'Committee on American Opinion and the British Empire', 30 December 1942.
11. PRO: *FO 930/514*, 'Memorandum by the FO on Propaganda Directed Against British Commonwealth' by M. Cook.
12. PRO: *FO 930/497*, 'Minute by J. Pilcher', 19 October 1946.

13. PRO: *FO 953/136*, 'Memorandum from the Middle East Information Department', 2 June 1948.
14. PRO: *FO 953/136*, 'Minute by Bradsaw', 8 May 1950.
15. See IOR: *L/I/1/1227*, 'Extract from letter by the India Office', 4 July 1947.
16. IOR: *L/I/1/1227*, 'Publicity in the British Commonwealth and Empire. Note by the Joint Secretary', circulated by J.A.R. Pimlott, 20 February 1944.
17. For a discussion of the proposal to establish a chair in colonial history in an American university, see PRO: *CO 875/19/17*.
18. PRO: *CO 875/15/11*, 'W.J. Turner to Lord Elton', 12 January 1942.
19. See PRO: *CO 875/14/11* for a discussion MOI sponsorship of publications.
20. PRO: *FO 930/479*, 'Official Committee on Government Information Services. The British Council' by B.D. Fraser, 20 December 1945.
21. PRO: *FO 953/136*, 'A.A. Dudley to K.W. Blackburne', 28 June 1948.
22. Mitchell (1955) pp. 21–2.
23. Harlow (1944) pp. 35 and 37.
24. Hodson (1948) p. 100.
25. Hailey (1943) p. 10.
26. *Daily Telegraph*, 29 July 1954, Crocker (1947) p. 138 and W.H. Ingrams 'Communist prospects in East and Central Africa', CO Confidential Print no. 1180, 1953 in PRO: *CO 879/157*.
27. Hailey (1943) p. 10 and Burns (1957) p. 62.
28. See M. Perham, 'African Facts and American Criticisms', *Foreign Affairs*, vol. 22, April 1944, pp. 447–8, R. Hinden, 'Socialism and the Colonial World' in Creech-Jones (1959) p. 13 and Creech-Jones 'The labour party and Colonial Policy 1945–51' in Creech-Jones (1959) p. 23.
29. See Hailey (1943) pp. 8–9, Harlow (1944) p. 16 and PRO: *CO 537/3746*, 'Minute from Rees-Williams to Lloyd', 28 May 1948.
30. Crocker (1947) p. 138. A contemporary example is provided by Sked who dismisses imperialism as a 'red-herring' in one breathtaking aside. See Sked (1989) p. 19.
31. See Perham, 'African facts ...', p. 449.
32. Koebner and Schmidt (1964) p. 282
33. Lipset (1963) p. 83.
34. Dance (1969) p. 33.
35. Indeed some of the most eloquent apologies for the British Empire are authored by Americans. In one of the most widely read books on the subject, Emerson writes: 'A plausible case can, however be made from the proposition that the future will look back upon overseas imperialism of recent centuries, less in terms of its sins of exploitation, and discrimination, than as the instrument by which the spiritual, scientific, and material

revolution which began in Western Europe with the Renaissance was spread to the rest of the world.' See Emerson (1960) p. 6.

36. Kohn (1966) p. 126.
37. Arendt (1967) p. 133.
38. Aron (1959) pp. 4–7.
39. Aron (1978) p. 221.
40. Bell (1980) p. 191.
41. Emerson (1960) p. 6.
42. PRO: *INF/ 1/559*, 'Comments on Overseas Planning Committee. West African Plan on the 1st October 1944', by MOI.
43. See T.E. Utley, 'The Imperialist Tradition', *Corona*, December 1953.
44. Feuer (1986) p. 112.
45. Burns (1957) pp. 28, 29, 34, 35.
46. See for example PRO: *FO 953/694*, 'Circular no. 078. Colonial Publicity' by K.G. Younger, 10 July 1950.
47. R. Emerson, 'The Character of American Interest in Africa' in Goldschmit (1958) p. 17.
48. Bell (1980) p. 206.
49. B.W. Jackson, 'Britain's Imperial Legacy', *Foreign Affairs*, vol. 35, no. 3, April 1957, p. 147.
50. D. Fromkin, 'The Strategy of Terrorism', *Foreign Affairs*, vol. 53, no. 4, July 1975, p. 683.
51. See Elton (1991) p. 45. Lord Beloff is cited by B.M. Gough, 'Pax Britannica: Peace, Force And World Power', *The Round Table*, no. 314, 1990, p. 169.
52. Emerson (1967) p. 2.
53. Blackburne (1976) p. 3 and Thomas (1981) p. 603, originally published in 1979.

Chapter 6: The Moral Rehabilitation of Imperialism

1. Elton in Gardiner (1990) p. 9. Charmley is cited in the *Independent on Sunday*, 10 January 1993.
2. Cited in the *Financial Times*, 1 November 1990.
3. Cited in *Living Marxism*, April 1991.
4. R.H. Jackson, 'Juridical Statehood in Africa', *Journal of International Affairs*, vol. 46, no. 1, 1992, p. 13.
5. Feuer (1986) p. 166.
6. B. Buzan, 'New Pattern of Global security', *International Affairs*, vol. 67, no. 3, July 1991, p. 440.
7. J. Casey, 'All Quiet on the Liberal Front', *Evening Standard*, 20 August 1990.
8. Peregrine Worsthorne, the former editor of the *Sunday Telegraph*, predicted the 'death' of the Third World and toasted the end of an era when the

'least important of Third World countries was courted, flattered and bribed by both sides'. See the *Sunday Telegraph*, 22 October 1989.

9. The *Wall Street Journal*, 12 July 1992.

10. D. Kellner, 'Critical Theory Today; Rewriting the Classics', *Theory, Culture and Society*, vol. 10, 1993, p. 46.

11. See 'Tribal nationalism, Balkanizing the World', *US News and World Report*, 28 December 1992.

12. See for example A.D. Smith, 'The Ethnic Sources of Nationalism', *Survival*, vol. 35, no. 1, 1993, p. 48.

13. D. Yankelovich, 'Foreign Policy after the Election', *Foreign Affairs*, Fall 1992, p. 9.

14. 'Editorial', the *Washington Post*, 17 December 1992.

15. See *Newsweek*, 21 June 1993,

16. See Smith, 'The Ethnic Sources …', *op. cit.*, p. 55.

17. See F.M. Deng, 'Africa and the New World Dis-order. Rethinking Colonial Borders', *The Brookings Review*, Spring 1993, pp. 34 and 35.

18. Davidson (1992) p. 247.

19. Ibid., p. 85.

20. Ibid., p. 73.

21. The only difference between the two points of view is that whereas Davidson romanticises, the colonial official demonises Africa's past. It is interesting to note that Kathryn Tidrick, an ardent defender of the British Empire, takes Davidson to task precisely on this point. Tidrick criticises Davidson's idealisation of Africa's past, particularly in relation to the Asante political system: 'nowhere is it mentioned that within this exemplary polity human sacrifice was practised on a terrific scale, or that the Asante owed their pre-eminence in wealth among their neighbours to their control of the slave trade'. See K. Tidrick, 'Who's to Blame?', *London Review of Books*; 25 February 1993.

22. See for example P. Landell-Mills, 'Governance, Cultural Change, and Empowerment', the *Journal of Modern African Studies*, 30, 4, 1992, p. 567.

23. Ahmad (1992) pp. 34–5.

24. I.L. Claude Jr., 'The Tension Between Principle and Pragmatism in International Relations', *Review of International Studies*, vol. 19, no. 3, July 1993, pp. 223–4 and 226.

25. W. Pfaff, 'Redefining World Power', *Foreign Affairs*, vol. 70, no. 1, p. 34.

26. J. Mayall, 'Non-Intervention, Self-Determination and the New World Order', *International Affairs*, vol. 67, no. 3, July 1991, p. 422.

27. J. Herbst, 'Challenges to Africa's Boundaries in the New World Order', *Journal of International Affairs*, vol. 46, no. 1, 1992, p. 17 and P. Hassner 'Beyond Nationalism and Internationalism: Ethnicity and World Order', *Survival*, vol. 35, no. 2, p. 62.

28. R.H. Jackson, 'Juridical Statehood in Sub-Saharan Africa', *Journal of International Affairs*, vol. 46, no. 1, 1992, p. 13.

29. R.I. Rotberg, 'The Clinton Administration and Africa', *Current History*, May 1993, p. 194.

30. The *Independent on Sunday*, 12 May 1991.

31. M. Woollacott, 'The Road from Iraq and Ruin', the *Guardian*, 29 July 1991.

32. Hobson (1988) (originally published in 1902) pp. 196–7.

33. ODA (1991) p. 1.

34. Feuer (1986) p. 1.

35. S. Zielonka, 'Europe's Security', *International Affairs*, vol. 67, no. 1, p. 131. For an elaborated version of this thesis, see Kennedy (1993).

36. K.R. Holmes, 'New World Disorder: A Critique of the United Nations', *Journal of International Affairs*, vol. 46, no. 2, 1993, p. 325.

37. T. Clancy and R. Seitz, 'Five Minutes Past Midnight – and Welcome to the Age of Proliferation', *National Interest*, no. 26, Winter 1991–2, p. 6.

38. B. Buzan, 'New Patterns of Global Security', *International Affairs*, July 1991, p. 445.

39. T. Rosenberg, 'Beyond Elections', *Foreign Policy*, no. 84, Fall 1991, p. 72.

40. 'Fighting the Unholy War', the *National review*, 19 July 1993, p. 14.

41. Cited in the *Washington Post*, 4 April 1993.

42. See K. Mahbubani, 'The West and the Rest', the *National Interest*, Summer 1992.

43. Buzan, *op. cit.*, p. 447.

44. M. Almond, 'Europe's Immigration Crisis', the *National Interest*, Fall 1992, no. 29, p. 53.

45. *Dernieres Nouvelles D'Alsace*, 21 August 1993.

46. W.S. Lind, 'Defending Western Culture', *Foreign Policy*, no. 84, Fall 1991, pp. 47 and 45.

47. Kennedy (1993) p. 46.

Select Bibliography

Ahmad, A. (1992) *In Theory: Classes, Nations, Literatures* (London: Verso).

Arendt, H. (1967) *Origins of Totalitarianism* (London: George Allen and Unwin).

Aron, R. (1959) Imperialism and Colonialism: The Seventeenth Montague Burton Lecture (Leeds: University of Leeds).

Aron, R. (1978) *Politics and History* (New York: The Free Press).

Bagehot, W. (1872) *Physics and Politics* (London: Henry S. King & Co.).

Bell, D. (1980) *Sociological Journeys* (London: Heinemann).

Blackburne, K. (1976) *Lasting Legacy: A History of British Colonialism* (London: Johnson Publications).

Bradley, K. (1966) *Once a District Officer* (London: Macmillan).

Buell, R.L. (1965) *The Native Problem in Africa*, vols. 1 and 2 (London: Frank Cass & Co.).

Bull, H. and Watson, A. eds. (1984) *The Expansion of International Society* (Oxford: Clarendon Press).

Bullock, A. (1991) *Hitler and Stalin: Parallel Lives* (London: Harper Collins).

Burns, Sir A. (1957) *In Defence of Colonies* (London: Macmillan).

Carr, E.H. (1941) *Nationalism and After* (London: Macmillan).

Creech-Jones, A.J. ed. (1959) *New Fabian Colonial Essays* (London: The Hogarth Press).

Crocker, W.J. (1947) *On Governing Colonies* (London: Macmillan).

Crocker, W.J. (1949) *Self-Government for the Colonies* (London: Macmillan).

Dance, E.H. (1969) *History the Betrayer: A Study in Bias* (London: Hutchinson).

Davidson, B. (1992) *The Black Men's Burden: Africa and the Curse of the Nation State* (London: James Currey).

Deletant, D. and Hanak, H. eds. (1988) *Historians as Nation Builders: Central and South East Europe* (London: Macmillan).

Despres, L.A. (1967) *Cultural Pluralism and Nationalist Politics in British Guiana* (Chicago: Rand McNally).

Dicey, A.V. (1905) *Lectures on the Relation Between Law and Public Opinion in England During the Nineteenth Century* (London: Macmillan).

Dryhurst, N.F. ed. (1919) *Nationalities and Subject Races: Report of a Conference held in Caxton Hall, Westminister, June 28–30, 1916* (London: P.S. King & Son).

Durkheim, E. (1964) *The Division of Labour in Society* (New York: The Free Press).

Echenberg, M. (1991) *Colonial Conscripts: The Tirailleurs senegalais in French West Africa, 1857–1960* (London: James Currey).

Elton, G.R. (1991) *Return to Essentials: Some Reflections on the Present State of Historical Study* (Cambridge: Cambridge University Press).

Emerson, R. (1960) *From Empire to Nation: The Rise to Self-Assertion of Asian and African Peoples* (Cambridge, Mass: Harvard University Press).

Emerson, R. (1967) *Africa and the United States Policy* (Englewood Cliffs, New York: Prentice-Hall).

Evans-Pritchard, E.E. (1965) *Theories of Primitive Religion* (Oxford: Clarendon Press).

Fanon, F. (1970) *Toward the African Revolution* (Harmondsworth: Pelican Books).

Feuer, L. (1986) *Imperialism and the Anti-Imperialist Mind* (Buffalo, New York: Prometheus Books).

Fitzgerald, F. (1979) *America Revisited* (Boston: Little Brown).

Fukuyama, F. (1992) *The End of History and the Last Man* (New York: The Free Press)

Füredi, F. (1989) *The Mau Mau War in Perspective* (London: James Currey).

Füredi, F. (1992) *Mythical Past, Elusive Future* (London: Pluto Press).

Füredi, F. (1994) *Colonial Wars and the Politics of Third World Nationalism* (London: I.B. Tauris).

Furnivall, J.S. (1948) *Colonial Policy and Practice: A Comparative Study of Burma and Netherlands India* (Cambridge: The University Press).

Gardiner, J. ed. (1990) *The History Debate* (London: Collins & Brown).

Gifford, P. and Louis, Wm.R. eds. (1982) *The Transfer of Power in Africa: Decolonisation, 1940–1960* (New Haven: Yale University).

Gifford, P. and Louis, Wm. R. eds. (1988) *Decolonisation and African Independence: The Transfers of Power, 1960–1980* (New Haven: Yale University Press).

Ginsberg, M. (1964) *The Psychology of Society* (London: Methuen).

Griswold, A.W. (1966) *The Far Eastern Policy of the United States* (New Haven: Yale University Press).

Grundy, K.W. (1983) *Soldiers Without Politics: Blacks in the South African Armed Forces* (Berkeley: University of California Press).

Gurtov, M. (1974) *The United States Against the Third World: Antinationalism and Intervention* (New York: Praeger).

Hailey, Lord (1943) *The Future of Colonial Peoples* (Oxford: Oxford University Press).

Hailey, Lord (1957) *An African Survey* (Oxford: Oxford University Press).

Haines, C.F. ed. (1955) *Africa Today* (Baltimore: The John Hopkins Press).

Hammond, D. and Jablow, A. (1970) *The Africa That Never Was* (New York: Twayne Publishers).

Harlow, V. (1944) *The British Colonies* (Oxford: Oxford University Press).

Hayes, C.J.H. (1926) *Essays on Nationalism* (New York: Macmillan).

Herskovits, M.J. (1967) *The Myth of the Negro Past* (Boston: Beacon Press).

Herz, F. (1951) *Nationality in History and Politics* (London: Routledge and Kegan Paul).

Hinden, R. ed. (1944) *Fabian Colonial Essays* (Oxford: Oxford University Press).

Hobsbawn, E.J. (1990) *Nations and Nationalism since 1780: Programme, Myth, Reality* (Cambridge: Cambridge University Press).

Hobson, J.A. (1901) *The Psychology of Jingoism* (London: Grant Richards).

Hobson, J.A. (1988) *Imperialism: A Study* (London: Unwin Hyman).

Hodgkin, T. (1957) *Nationalism in Colonial Africa* (New York: New York University Press).

Hodson, H.V. (1948) *Twentieth Century Empire* (London: Faber and Faber).

Hroch, M. (1985) *Social Preconditions of National Revival in Europe* (Cambridge: Cambridge University Press).

Hughes, E.C. and Hughes, H.M. (1981 reprint) *Where Peoples Meet: Racial and Ethnic Frontiers* (Westport: Greenwood Press).

Hyam, R. (1992) *The Labour Government and the End of Empire 1945–51, Part I, High Policy and Administration* (London: HMSO).

Kamenka, E. ed. (1976) *Nationalism: The Nature and Evolution of an Idea* (London: Edward Arnold).

Kennedy, P. (1993) *Preparing For the Twenty-First Century* (London: Harper Collins)

Koebner, R. and Schmidt, H.D. (1964) *Imperialism: The Story and Significance of a Political Word 1840–1964* (Cambridge: Cambridge University Press).

Kohn, H. (1932) *Nationalism in the Hither East* (London: George Routledge and Sons).

Kohn, H. (1946) *The Idea of Nationalism* (New York: Macmillan).

Kohn, H. (1966) *Political Ideologies of the Twentieth Century* (New York: Harper and Row).

Lansing, R. (1921) *The Peace Negotiations* (New York: Macmillan).

Laski, H.J. (1932) *Nationalism and the Future of Civilization* (London: Watts and Co.).

Le Bon, G. (1990) reprint *The Crowd: The Study of the Popular Mind* (Dunwoody, Georgia: Norman & Berg Publisher).

Lippman, W. (1934) *Public Opinion, 4th Edition* (New York: Macmillan).

Lipset, M. (1963) *Political Man: The Social Bases of Politics* (Garden City, NY: Anchor Books).

Lowell, A.L. (1913) *Public Opinion and Popular Government* (New York: Longmans, Green and Co.).

Macmillan, W.M. (1949) *Africa Emergent* (Harmondsworth: Penguin).

Mahoney, R.D. (1983) *JFK: Ordeal in Africa* (Columbia: Columbia University)

Malinowski, B. (1938) *Methods of Study of Culture Contact in Africa* (Oxford: Oxford University Press).

Malinowski, B. (1945) *The Dynamics of Culture Change: An Inquiry into Race Relations in Africa* (New Haven: Yale University Press).

Matthews, B. (1926) *Study in the Problem of Race* (London: Edinburgh House Press).

Mayall, J. (1990) *Nationalism and International Society* (Cambridge: Cambridge University Press).

Mayo, K. (1927) *Mother India* (London: Jonathan Cape).

McGhee, G. (1983) *Envoy to the Middle World* (New York: Harper Row).

Meyer, F.S. ed. (1965) *The African Nettle* (New York: The John Day Co.).

Michels, R. (1949) *Political Parties* (Glencoe, Illinois: Free Press).

Mockaitis, T.R. (1990) *British Counterinsurgency, 1919–60* (London: Macmillan).

Morsy, M. (1984) *North Africa 1800–1900* (London: Longman).

Myrdal, G. (1960) *Asian Drama* (London: Allen Lane).

Namier, L.B. (1962) *Vanished Supremacies* (Harmondsworth: Penguin).

Noer (1988) *Black Liberation: The US and White Rule in Africa, 1948–68* (Columbia, Missouri: Missouri University Press).

Nye, R. (1975) *The Origins of Crowd Psychology and the Crisis of Mass Democracy in the Third Republic* (London: Sage).

Ostrogorski, M. (1902) *Democracy and the Organisation of Political Parties* (New York: Macmillan).

Overseas Development Agency (ODA) (1991) *Children by Choice, Not Chance* (London: ODA).

Park, R.E. (1950) *Race and Culture* (Glencoe, Illinois: The Free Press).

Perham, M. (1962) *The Colonial Reckoning* (London: Reith Lectures).

Porter, A.N. and Stockwell, A.J. eds. (1989) *British Imperial Policy and Decolonisation, 1938–64*, vol. 1 (London: Macmillan).

Richmond, A.H. (1955) *The Colour Problem: A Study of Racial Relations* (Harmondsworth: Penguin).

Rosebery, Lord (1900) *Questions of Empire* (London: Arthur L. Humphreys).

Royal Institute of International Affairs (RIIA) (1937) *The Colonial Problem: A Report by a Study Group of Members of the RIIA* (Oxford: Oxford University Press).

Royal Institute of International Affairs (RIIA) (1939) *Nationalism, A Report by a Study Group of Members of the RIIA* (Oxford: Oxford University Press).

Said, E.W. (1985) *Orientalism* (London: Penguin).

Sked, A. (1989) *Britain's Decline* (Oxford: Basil Blackwell).

Smith, A.D. (1990) *National Identity* (London: Penguin).

Snyder, L.L. (1989) *Race: A History of Modern Ethnic Theories* (New York: Longman, Green and Co.).

Staniland, M. (1991) *American Intellectuals and African Nationalists 1905–1970* (New Haven: Yale University Press).

Stonequist, E.V. (1961) *The Marginal Man: A Study in Personality and Culture Conflict* (New York: Russell and Russell Inc.).

Thomas, H. (1981) *The Unfinished History of the World* (London: Pan Books).

Tidrick, K. (1990) *Empire and the English Character* (London: I.B. Tauris).

Townshend, C. (1986) *Britain's Civil Wars: Counterinsurgency in the Twentieth Century* (London: Faber and Faber).

Toynbee, A.J. (1948) *Civilisation on Trial* (Oxford: Oxford University Press).

Turner, G.H. ed. (1923) *Public Opinion and World Peace* (Washington DC: ILCA).

Wallas, G. (1961) *Human Nature in Politics* (London: Constable).

Walsby, H. (1947) *The Domain of Ideology* (Glasgow: William Maclellan).

Westermann, D. (1939) *The African Today and Tomorrow* (Oxford: Oxford University Press).

Index